Eely

*To Jacqui,
All good wishes!
Steve Ely*

Eely

Steve Ely

Longbarrow Press

Published in 2024 by
Longbarrow Press
76 Holme Lane
Sheffield
S6 4JW

www.longbarrowpress.com

Printed by T.J. Books Ltd,
Padstow, Cornwall

All rights reserved

Poems © Steve Ely 2024
Jacket artwork © P.R. Ruby 2024
Jacket design © Brian Lewis 2024

ISBN 978-1-906175-48-1

First edition

Contents

Eel

11   Eel

/ˈiːlaɪ/

- 49   Infangtheof
- 51   Inglnz Dreamin
- 56   Dads at Lads
- 57   The Leeds & District ASA
- 57   *WMC Crawl*
- 57   *Any Other Business*
- 59   */ˈstiːvnz/ Rod*
- 60   *The Barkstone Ash & Skyrac Volunteers*
- 62   Gibbets
- 62   *Predator Control*
- 62   *Vermin*
- 63   The Bridge
- 66   Plum
- 68   The Ship
- 71   John's & Sam's
- 73   /ˈstiːvn/
- 73   *Jimmy Deadbait*
- 74   *The Serenade of the Black Dwarfs*
- 75   *Jimmy the Tiger*
- 76   */ˈstiːvn ˈiːlaɪ/ is a puff*
- 77   *Jörmungandr*
- 78   *marvelous weraal origin story*
- 80   The American Mink

82 Bollwurz
82   *Maisbeli*
83   *Idlæ*
84   *Hæðfeld*
85   *Winwædfeld*
86 Quo Warranto?

eely

89 *forwyrd*
90 body of dark
91 behold the head of a traitor
92 porzana
93 bloodspoor
94 pull down thy vanity
95 the patience & faith of the saints
96 the cross of a frog
97 ex nihilo ad nihilum
98 moira
99 10^{-43}
100 i do in all honesty love this world
101 jubilee
102 ararita

Eelysium

105 Eeliptical Fencentricities
105   *Storegga*
107   *Elverkonge*
107   *Morimarusa*
109   *The Enthronement Feast of Archbishop George Neveel*
111   *Girvij*

112	Eeldorado
112	*Eelizardbirth*
114	*Baseeliske*
115	*Corneelius*
116	*Hatfeeld Chace*
119	*The Great Leveel*
121	Eelimentary Tractaet van Dijckagie
121	*Tyranipocrit*
122	*Balby Carr Pastoreel*
125	*Privy Counceel*
126	*Sea-worm*
128	*Commissioners of Sewers*
130	Eelkonoklastes
130	*Filth as thou art*
132	*Grendeel*
133	*The Black Mirror*
135	*The Ruin of Heorot*
136	*Suspiria Regeelia*
138	Enuma Eelysh
138	*Gods of Storm & Abyss*
139	*The Burbots of Guthlac*
140	*Pantaneel*
144	*Dreams of Sturgeon*
147	*Πάντα Ρεελ*
149	Notes and Glossary
184	Acknowledgements

Eel

In the Subtropical Convergence Zone
of the southern Sargasso, over the edge of the Nares Abyssal,
south-east of the Bermuda Ridge, snow is rising
in the water column from fifteen hundred feet.
Somewhere in Tethys' salty darkness,
in spurts of milt and billowing roe, eels
are birthing their posterity, a spore-storm of eggs
in uncountable centillions, each buoyed
on its micron of oil. The embryos float
in the Miocene water like dust motes
caught in a shaft of light, and ascending
through the photocline, join the thermonuclear
microplankton of the drifting epipelagic.

In the eighteen-degree water, hatching—
it is hypothesised—takes place after two days
of embryonic growth, after which emerges
the pinhead imago—veined, elongate,
a leaf of transparent white willow—*leptocephalus*,
the larval form of anguilla, absorbing its yolk-sac
for ten or twelve days, lengthening daily
by micrometres, gaining weight daily in microgrammes,
until a fortnight after hatching, the size
of a sand-grain or emphatic full-stop,
it unhinges its tiny, gaping jaws,
fangs half as long as its head, and hunts
in the eutrophic blizzard, seizing diatoms,
dinoflagellates, polyethylene microbeads,
fuelling-up for the thirty-month long haul,
Sargasso to the Biscay Abyssal.

Sargasso, a bright lens of brine sitting light
on the freeze of the Antarctic Bottoms,
herded to a hump by the North Atlantic Gyre.
The desert sea, life confined to its turbulent edges,
the highways of the eel, and the surface rafts
of drifting sargassum from which it takes its name.
The graveyard sea, swallower of troopships
and Grumman Avengers, where the drowned
float forever in zombied suspension
and the albatross rots on the mirror.
Columbus struck his prow right through it,
en route to the New World's plunder,
but he liked the Sargasso—*blue as the sky
in Andalusia, fragrant as the air in Seville*—
the garbage sea, where the plastic of three continents
forms mats the breadth of Spain.

South of the plastic, offshore from Puerto Rico,
leptocephali ride on the Antilles current.
Feeding at night in the epipelagic, they in daylight
descend to the dark of Deep Scattering,
a phototaxic flight from the light and the deaths
that lurk there: harpooning cnidarians,
the grip-claws of krill, the lit jaws of the lanternfish—
devoured in centillions, centillions riding still.
A month or so since hatching, the size
of an April tadpole, they move in the plankton
like Pac-Man, simple machines of growth
and devouring, deliverers of the savage telos
written in their genes. They drift with the current,
making five or fifteen miles each day,
beyond Grand Bahama to the Blake Escarpment,
where the Florida current blows out from the strait
on the plume of Deepwater Horizon.
There, between Andros Island and Biscayne Bay,
it courses into the racing Antilles,
to form the Gulf Stream, a roaring salt river
hurtling north on the edge of the American
continental shelf, its estuaries of blight:
oestrogen-saturated sewage, methamphetamine
neurotoxins, chromosome warping
neonicotinoid run-off. The leptocephali soak it up,
and tumble to Hatteras with the flotsam
of the current—single-use Canaveral
space junk, the strip mall's car-tossed,
fast-food trash and radioactive manatees.

At Diamond Shoals, the Stream swerves north-east,
beyond Chesapeake Bay and the New York Bight
to the sea lanes over the Hudson Canyon.
There, in the diesel rumble of supertankers
and Liberian-registered Panamax freighters,
the leptocephali rise and fall, oblivious
to the onslaught: swarming capelin,
hoovering humpbacks, ravening hydrozoans—
CO_2 and CH_4, slicks of tank-flushed crude.
Every second of their journey is the first day
of the Somme, the annihilating batteries unrelenting,
but blithe the wide battalions ride, and redden their blades
in the ancient slaughter. Each life is built
from the bones of a billion dead,
and in their deaths are the murdered risen;
as long as the ocean circulates, eels
will find their way—but maybe, as the ice melts,
the current itself will stutter and dive,
and the larva slide to extinction's deeps
on the shelves of Atlantic's Niño.
For now, they travel, and the broad shoals sail
off Nova Scotia and enter the Grand Banks'
desolate plateau, its right whale wrecks
and trawled-out, cod-less seas. Spectres
wail in the infrasonic, and ping their griefs
off the sonar's screen: the live-plucked,
live-boiled auks of Funk, exterminated Beothuk
and the cleared and fly-tipped Gaels of Uist—
Whigs and Tories, their captains, crowns and thrones.

At Flemish Cap, the Trade Winds falter,
and the Labrador current pushes the Stream
out into the open ocean, where the salt river runs
in the zephyral flow of the thermohaline
North Atlantic Drift. Still bearing its load
of feeding leptocephali, the current fans out
through the lit pelagic in a delta of blooming phytoplankton
that stretches from Iceland to Western Sahara.
The central mass drifts east-north-east,
between the Azores and the Altair Seamount,
until west of Biscay and the Celtic Sea,
it passes over the grazing heights of the Porcupine Abyssal,
where, harried by cetorhines and schools
of swarming mackerel, the leptocephali
continue to travel and grow, rippling spearheads
of foliate gelatine, glittering in the half-lit heave
like a shoal of shredded cling-film.

By August, the wandering larval eels
have arrived at the edge of the European shelf,
where they halt in the deeps off the Porcupine Seabight.
Now the length of an autumn stickleback,
they can grow no more and stop feeding.
For two-and-a half years, helpless drifters
on the gyre, they somehow drop invisible anchors
and hold against the flow. Here, in the twilit mesopelagic,
in the chemotaxic outflow of Shannon,
Severn and Seine, they hang in the heft
of the catalytic waters and begin the first metamorphosis.
Increased respiration metabolises fat
and excretes excess water; zigzag myomeres
harden to muscle and bone. Each polythene ribbon

shrinks to a rubbery, see-through sea-snake,
thinner than an iPhone charging cable,
the length of my little finger—*glass eel*,
the microcosmic perfect form of the yellow eel
in its cave. An army of billions, stacked
offshore in the buffeting Drift and arrowed against the flow,
waiting for the occult sign that will herald
the surge into continental waters, each travelling
in the flexural power of its new undulatory wiggle.

Under the New Year's wintry constellations,
the glass eels begin their ascent.
Between the Porcupine Bank and the Goban Spur,
they emerge from submarine, deep-sea darkness
into the sunlit shallows of the Celtic Sea.
No longer the helpless, tropic flotsam
of the blown and thermohaline gyre,
they travel under their own steam, setting course
with the sextant of their mystic DNA.
Deep Scattering cannot hide them now,
from the predatory haddock and whiting,
sea bass, flounder and squid, so they travel by night
and bury themselves in the seabed's silts by day,
swimming against the tides and currents,
magnetised to their destinies in the scent
of distant rivers. The estuaries of the west—
Gironde and Tagus, Shannon, Severn
and Seine—swallow them in billions; but billions more
track east along the Channel, in the rumbling
diesel effluent of the 'busiest sea lane in the world',
its freight of towering container ships,
the rise and swell of pearl-eyed refugees.

Onward they flow, making five or six miles daily:
over Hurd's Deep—where the MoD
dumped its phosgene shells and plutonium 239—
and the paleo-valleys and fossil meanders
of the Weichselian Glacial Maximum.
In the wreckage of Dunkirk and 1588,
they bury themselves among pieces-of-eight
and the little boat bones of drunken sailors.
The rivers of Wessex tempt some of them in,
but millions pass through Dover's straits
and into the German Sea. Once more they're changing,
darkening from head to tail, the glaze
becoming smoked and blurry—the glass eels
are transforming to *elvers*, gearing up for the move
into estuary and river, garbing themselves
in the colour of mud that for years will be their element.

Thames and Medway draw in their loads,
as do the southern fenland rivers,
but the vanguard of the shoal swims north,
some crossing to Rhine and Skaggerak,
the fjords of western Norway.
Millions more track the Danelaw's coasts,
in the lukewarm sump of the muck-brown seaside sea.
Too deep for Bempton's travelling gannets,
flounders gulp them from the silts and gadoids
take their quotas. Past oil and gas rigs,
the trunks of turbines, in the estuarine scent
of *nearly there*, they straggle along the Lincolnshire coast
past Skeggy Butlins and Chapel St. Leonards,
to Ívarr's gap between Cleethorpes and Spurn,
where a column splits off and enters the Humber—
the end of their three-year saltwater journey.

In the lanes where the pilots ply their trade,
the elvers divide on submarine shoals
to form cordons off Lindsey and York.
Armoured in mucus and toxic blood
against the hypotonic water and its pathogenic load,
they battle upstream in the brawling spate
of Three Ridings and Five Boroughs.
Harried by conger, crab and mullet,
herons and plunging grebes, the northern cordon
inches forward, under the mud-bank's steep phragmites,
past Skeffling Clays and Sunk Island Sands,
to the wharves and piers of the Port of Hull,
where they hide from the light in the dredgings of Empire:
bright litter of cod-skulls and cobbles of steam-coal,
uncoopered casks of rendered spermaceti.

Springtide sucks the elvers from the silts
and shoulders back the Humber. They ride
on the roar of the muscular bore to the sands
of Whitton Island, where the cordon splits once more.
A southern contingent is channelled mid-river
and into the Mercian Trent; the northern stream
flows along Faxfleet's shores and enters
the Ouse at the Blacktoft Channel. Great Ouse,
Eiríkr's dragon-prowed highway of commerce and blood,
where the Nassau-registered FRI Marlin
rides in the wake of the Humber Pride,
its cargo of half-pigs and Immingham diesel.
In the dark-moon growl of turning screws,
the elvers scale the wapentakes' flow
in a shock of suspended glyphosate
and the '62's condensed benzene.

At the reedbed's edge, black-headed gulls
come flocking and dipping; otters dive
in the turbid bounty and bitterns fill their crops.
Men with hand nets send the long shoal shattering.
A column along the Laxton shore straggles
upriver all summer, past the Port of Goole
and Howdendyke, to the confluence with Aire.
From there they'll travel north and west
into the PRIVATE salmon and brown trout streams
of Northfield's Tory sports day—Dales, Wolds and Moors.
But pressed against the western curve of Old Goole's
hooked meander, a depleted hundred-thousand ride
beneath the flood-wall's reedy strandline,
through sunken junk of fly-tipped prams
and bridge-tossed shopping trolleys.
There, between the Co-op and Vermuyden Terrace,
they pass into the Dutchman's canalised Don
and the drained and pumped, grid-linear waters
of the powerhouse West Riding, its bypasses
and business parks, sprawls of mortgaged housing.
Barely a cordon, hardly a shoal, they move into the kingdom
of the Amazon Fulfilment Centre, its clear-fell
devastation of investment, jobs and growth.

In the zero-hour run-off of link roads
and logistics, the elvers travel in dark solution,
past Decoy Farm and Rawcliffe Bridge,
under the M18. Below the floodbank
at Greenland Farm, anglers dip their poles.
Each elver's a little eel now, a *bootlace*,
the length and girth of an HB pencil,
knotting in slime on the brandlinged hook

in the *yellow eel* livery of those seventies Ulleskelf years—
newt-brown uppers from nose-to-tail,
bacon-rind belly, flanks tinged with yellowy-green.
Recall the snake-head's underbite,
its saurian gaze and billowing gape
of breathing; those weird procellariid nostrils,
and the eye—bronze iris, black pupil,
a gaze from the depths of the Oligocene Tethys.
The hook's taken too deep and cannot be disgorged,
save with scissors or decapitating knife—
drops lopped into river, vanishes in the flow.

The little eels swim past Went Green sluice
to the cormorant fields of Fishlake parish,
before crossing the cobbles of the submerged ford
to Bramwith on the oxbowed ings.
From here, most swim due south to Danum,
and beyond to the moorland heads of the river.
But in the shadow of the clap-cold cooling towers
of National Power's defunct Thorpe Marsh,
a trickle veers west through a hanging wooden floodgate,
exiting through the levee of the canalised Don
to pass between the levees of the canalised Old Ea Beck.

They don't know where they're going.
Not like the river-born, anadromous salmon,
homing upstream to their natal redds
along the madeleine scent of the current.
These eels were born in a continent of ocean
and their parents delivered unto that vastness
on mindless, predictable, pot-luck currents
from Iceland, Belgium, Tunisia, Spain.

Reliable gyres steer the rudderless broods
to their Palaearctic landfall, where the elvers
ascend any freshwater outflow, from Hvita
on the Arctic Circle to Gueguerat
under the African Tropic of Cancer.
Ea's straggling cordon got here by chance,
their kin devoured by a hundred different *it'll do* rivers,
Al Khatt, Guadiana and Abhainn Mhor,
the big gapes of Tagus, Severn and Loire.

They don't know where they are.
The lit shallows run tepid but the bottoms
are cool and dark. The feeding is rich
and easy—roach fry, leeches, bivalves,
worms—so each little eel anchors
and runs its Miocene program: hide from light,
hunt at night, grow long and thick and fat.
The Ea is perfect, or would be, were it not
for the big eels—some three feet long
and thick as a man's wrist—long-rooted
in their benthic plots, snapping them up,
sending them scooting upcurrent.

Thus the little eels travel, driven deeper
into the drainage, each seeking a plot of their own.
Some strike it lucky, and courtesy of cormorant,
heron or otter, find vacant caves
under Marsh Lane bridge, just a hundred yards on
from the floodgate. The rest trek forward,
past Sickle Croft at Thorpe-in-Balne
and the power station settling ponds,
where huge pike haul down half-grown swans

and full-grown crested grebes. There, in midnight
drenchings of summer thunder, some wriggle
through the grass of the sodden embankment
and squirm into the roots of the warm ponds'
deep phragmites. They'll trust blind chance
in the prowling murk and live on jack and fry.

From the Don to the A1(M), Ea flows
in its V between flat-topped mounds
dredged and piled by long-arm Komatsu crawlers.
The silts are dumped to dry out in the sun,
with their writhing collateral of suffocating eels.
In the filth and smashed flag, under squalls
of gulls and chancing crows, the survivors persist
in their straggling ascent, labouring the shallows
between moated Tilts and the ruin of Bentley Colliery,
its unpumped workings black with coal
and seams of dungeoned eels. What species
will they become there? What have they become
already?—the legend of the Bentley Worm,
roaming the anthracite bowels of the earth
starved on the firedamp ghosts of miners,
emerging each Walpurgis Night from the depths
of the Welfare pit-pond, seizing tribute
from the ranks of the High Street's drunks
and the graveyard's coked-up, shrieking children.

Below Bullcroft tips at Carcroft common,
the beck runs under Watling Street
past the ASDA superstore and B&Q,
between Richard's Hampole and Robin Hood's Well.
In the approach to the thundering culvert
under the Doncaster-Wakefield road,

the Ea becomes the Hampole dike,
and in a fly-tipped paddock below the landfill,
finds, for the first time, its natural meander:
staggers of alder and tangled willow,
tussock-topped, flood-sheared cliffs.
The eels rest up in rat-holes, hunt fry
in the willows' cool shade: until something
in the water, or in the coding of their genes,
sends them questing against the current—
another crawling culvert in the landfill's reek.
They exit to the light in a sheer-walled stream
between the London-Edinburgh railway line
and Stubbs Hall's leaky carp ponds:
blue shit seeping from chemical toilets,
cormorants dribbling lead. Rats feeding
from litter bins, discarded peg-side boilies.
The little eels slither in the meal deal flow
and enter an ocean of drifting rape
where the dikewater stinks like Roundup
and fitches—mink are patrolling the red-brick cave
under the shut-down colliery spur
of the shut-down Hull & Barnsley railway.
Darkness releases them into darkness,
the starless waters of Elmsall beck
in the stench of the Common End sewerage.
Now fifteen miles upstream from Don,
only a handful of eels remain of the shoal
that passed the Thorpe-in-Balne control gate.
Nowhere to go now; in three or four miles
the map's fine blue line will fritter
in a maze of spring-fed trickles in the fields
between Hemsworth and Kirkby.

But a quarter-mile beyond the sewerage,
in the flood-flattened rape below Lovatt's garage,
new water joins the flow—Frickley beck,
the barely-a-mile-long terminal flow
of a tangle of tiny dikes and springs that rise
from the clays between Watchley and Ringstone Hill.
A dozen or so divert and enter its current.
They wriggle along the flat-scraped silt
in the sheer-side drain of the embanked channel
and pass under the road to the ragwort horsefield
in the shadow of Frickley tips. Stridable stream,
meandering under the bankside hawthorns
in a foot or two of depth. Once a home
for water voles and nesting bankside moorhens:
that was before the mink. But even in this desultory trickle,
with its workaday load of pesticides
and annual blights of field-dumped pigshed slurry,
the waterworld's intact: you can still tickle trout,
and river fish flee before your bootsteps—
dace and gudgeon, bullhead and barbel,
the odd patrolling pike. And eels, of course,
buried under banks, in the clefts of rootballs,
wherever the beck finds a yard or so of depth.

At the tunnel-lip under the H&B spur,
only three from Sargasso remain to complete
their ascent. The downstream dredging
killed hundreds of eels and some of the new ones
took their vacant places. Herons prowl
this easy water, and mink work the pool
at the step of the tunnel, where the travelling eels
are forced to attempt a grass snake's slithering ascent.

Only one makes it through and into Frickley Park.
Here the beck widens and deepens for a stretch,
as the flow backs up at the arch of the tunnel.
The stream cuts across the pylon field
between banks of nettles and the bollarded stumps
of hawthorns. The surviving eel swims forward,
winding between the banks, seeking a plot
in which she can anchor for the next fifteen or twenty years.
She sniffs the waters with her periscope nostrils,
wriggles into root knots and debris-dams.
This stream has good feeding, bloodworm,
caddis and fry; but already there are eels here,
with gapes wide enough to swallow her skinny
nine inches whole; they loom from darkness,
lunging and biting, taking chunks from her caudal
and ventral fins, chasing her on upstream.

Where the beck is straightened along Frickley Lane
she crawls along the ballasted shallows
under a wall of gabioned limestone.
Here the waters flow fast and broken,
as the tumbling spate of Holywell beck
roars into the flow from a concrete pipe
and roils in its rumbling plunge pool.
The stones of the bridge the pipe replaced,
along with the swallow's nest, crusted to the ashlar,
were abandoned in the flow to cause this foaming turbulence.
The eel flashes under the feral white water
and slides into the flat-bottomed, deep-cut race
that glints through the lattice of slashed-back quick
a fathom below the lane. Hard-banks here,
no shelter—but shortly the stream begins to widen
and find a little depth: another pipe,

another plunge pool, at the gateless gap
facing Hooton Thorn Covert, on the point
of the nameless, fox-head wood. Waist-deep
and wide enough for a man to float on his back
like Jesus. The covert side grassy, unhedged;
the lane side flailed and splintered hawthorn,
 a sycamore's overhang gloom. She reaches the pipe-lip,
only inches above her surface-breaking head,
submerges and circles the pool. Beneath the pipe-drop's
trickle of fall, a dark eel rises, lunging
from the rubble towards her. She flicks off
in a plume of silt, and continues her circling
in the sycamore's shadow, snaking the caves
of the submarine rootball—rat smells,
trout smells, effluent from the Landrace piggery,
stinks of dead pigeon, pheasant and crow.
Bloodworm, caddis and fry. Eel smell—
but no incumbent eel. So, under the bank
of Frickley beck, by the gateless gap
at Hooton Thorn Covert, on the point
of the nameless fox-head wood, she reaches the end
of her forty-month journey. She knots her tail
in a crevice of the rootball and pokes out
her gape in a predatory billow of breathing.
Now she waits, and rests.

Sunday morning, twelfth of May, 2019: I pulled from the pool the eBay crab pot and saw her knotting in the sock. The first one I'd caught since the Ulleskelf bootlace of 1977—which I disgorged by lock-knife decapitation, the custom at the time. I unzipped her into the waiting bucket and skipped a beaming mile along the lane to the verge where I'd parked the car—they're still here!

The tank had been ready for a month, but the eels— in Went and Ea and Howell becks—weren't taking my Tesco fish-counter bait, and I started to wonder if their inexhaustible biomass had become exhausted already. But maybe the water was just too cold, or the whiffy sprats just too long dead. 48 x 18 x 15 inches, 200 hose-piped litres, bedded on one-inch polystyrene on top of the garage shoe-cupboard. Three inches of gravel, a cave of broken potsherds. Oxygenating Ranunculus, Elodea canadenis.

I tipped her in, and watched her circle in whiplash panic the walls of her glassy cage. 'Just for the summer,' I told her. 'Just for the poem. You'll be back in your pool by autumn.' And I flattened my palm against the glass in a gesture of reassurance. But that only made it worse, so I stepped back from the tank to remove my threat and watched from a perch on the dog crate. After a while she seemed to settle and peered out from her potsherd cave. 'Ella,' I said, and was mightily pleased with myself— until I remembered Mijbil and Toki, and Christian the Hugging Lion. So I stuck with the name I'd started to call her already—little eel.

After three days my little eel had made herself at home, poking her head out from under the potsherds and kneading her gills in a pleated billow of breathing. She didn't seem to mind me, unless I rearranged the furniture of the tank or lurched before the glass. I put in a red bulb, pulled up a stool, and watched. Mostly she'd just burrow in the substrate—a plunging whip-crack pluming silt, rattling the glass with gravel, then poke out her head from the stones: blank Miocene gaze, gaped underslung hook-jaw and that metronome billow of breathing. Sometimes in the dark-room darkness she'd loop her infinities over the gravels and snake to the top of the water. Once she stretched full-length along the pane and allowed me to tape her measurements: nineteen inches, thick as a garden hosepipe—so conceivably a he, even from the catchment's far extremity. But something seemed off about her yellow eel livery. The upperparts were a little too dark, and a bloom of bronze seemed to shine from her gills and neck. Not like I remembered from the Wharfe or the Went, or like the exemplars on Google Images. I put it down to natural variation, and brought her food.

I fed her every day. She was a picky eater, rejecting sprats and mackerel chunks, strips of beef and blocks of frozen shrimp—too dead, too foreign to her beck-raised habit. The live food I provided—bloodworm, mussels, tadpoles and fry, including an inch-long perfect pike—disappeared from the tank, but I never saw her make a kill, or caught her eating anything else but earthworms. She'd only take the big ones, the six-inch crawlers. I'd lower them slowly over her head. They'd be wriggling before her and suddenly   vanished —an echo of gulp, faint ripple in the water—Miocene gaze, gaped underslung hook-jaw, that metronome billow of breathing. She'd take three or four in quick succession, then nothing for two or three days or more, despite my efforts to tempt her. Tank bottom strewn with waving chironomids, limp streamers of bleached lumbricus.

Mid-June, her eating had become erratic and the gaps between feeding grew longer. Come July, she was fasting for weeks at a time. A whisper between my temples—*you're making her ill*—*take her back to her pool or you'll kill her.* I gazed for confirmation. She gazed right back—Miocene gaze, underslung hook-jaw, metronome billow of breathing. No telepathy, no communion. She lived her life in the jaws of a cormorant, and I was nothing but a heretic cormorant, one that toyed and would not kill, unaccountably parallel with her living. Miocene gaze, underslung hook-jaw, metronome billow of breathing.

By August she'd changed her skulking habit, and spent her days hanging tall in the tank, anchored in the gravel by the tail. And her yellow eel livery was definitely off— her back was dark, her belly pale, her gills were glinting foil—was she silvering? I couldn't be sure: I'd not seen a silver eel for 40 years, since Julius foul-hooked that storied two-pounder at Smeaton on the Went; so I dropped my eBay creel once more, to compare and contrast.

In the tank together, the difference was clear. The new eel was riverine yellowy-green. Little eel was transforming into her guillemot ocean livery. Maybe that's why her eating had become erratic—perhaps she'd begun to absorb her gut as she started her metamorphosis—though she bit out a chunk from the interloper before I took it back.

In August, she ate nothing at all. 'Let her go,' the whisper said. 'It's cruel to keep her confined in that tank in the gloom of the garage. She's pining for the length of the river, that's why she won't eat.' Anchored in the gravel, *billowing her breathing, fixed in that Miocene stare. Getting darker, paler and mackerel metallic and even her eyes were boggling larger. There was no doubt about it. In a month she'd be set to swim for Sargasso.*

So I netted her from the tank and tipped her in the bucket and walked the lane to the pool on the point of the fox-head wood: where I crouched in the shade of the overhang sycamore and prepared to empty her in; and where I hesitated, and touched her for the first time, sending her circling the bucket in panic; and so had to reassure her, explaining that I meant no harm, then and in the period of her kidnap and captivity. And I explained to her why I'd done what I'd done, and that I hoped she understood, and that she might remember me, because I would certainly remember her; and that maybe, someday, it might fall to either one of our fates to be called to help the other, in this world or the subtil world of spirit. So I said goodbye to my little eel, and emptied her into the culvert's plunge-pool, where she unwound down in the darkling waters and vanished in the caves of the sycamore's submarine rootball.

Late September dark moon. Thunderheads
massing and snarling. She stirs in her cave
in the sycamore rootball. Her black and silver skin is tight,
her rippling snake-flesh slick with gleaming fat.
She lifts her head and breathes the water,
kneading her long pectorals. Eyes like oversized
pilot goggles, clapped to the sides of her head,
rods supplanting cones in the second transformation.
She perceives only light and darkness now,
the spatial acuity of predatory vision
a redundant inefficiency: six thousand
black and fasting miles to the spawning grounds
of the southern Sargasso, over the edge of the Nares Abyssal,
south-east of the Bermuda Ridge.
She stretches her length from the submarine tangle
and tastes the turbulent, swollen waters—recoils
from dusk-light dimming overhead.
Winds restless through the maze of roots and snags.

Stacked cumulonimbus, blacked-out
constellations. Hammering rain, stripping
the beaten sycamores. Field drains foaming
with tilth in suspension. Beck risen to the arch
of the culvert pipe, leaf-litter corkscrewing
under the tunnel in a roaring Coriolis whirlpool.
She stretches again from her submarine rootball
to sniff in the whelming flow: Nitram, Roundup,
Viroxide Super, Supalyx equine mineral-lick—
the olfactory blur of migrating silver eels.
She loosens her tail and abandons her length
to the current—flung rope in the torrent,
hurtling with the debris in suspension—black blizzards
of leaves and broken-off branches, cannoning
bottles and tins. Flushed through culverts
and under bridges, bent forests of bulrush and torn-off
mats of flag, she's thundered across the inundated common
to the maelstrom confluence with Elmsall beck,
where a stubblefield lake is expanding upstream
in the whiff of the sewerage outflow,
eel stink tumbling blindly beside her,
grey froth of used condoms and sanitary towels.
Ghostly vortex of mewling black-head gulls.

Shot out from the H&B culvert like a cork,
she rides the torrent to Carcroft Common
where the Ea has broadened to thirty feet
and is overtopping its light industrial floodbanks.
Sodium streetlights glower in siling darkness,
but the pummelling current of black whitewater
is too strong to be resisted. She's swept on the surge
to the confluence with Don, sheer volume of flood
backing up at the pipe, a surface-breaking,

wrestling shoal of stymied silver eels—
but the gate's slammed open by the force of the flux
and the suck of the distant German Sea.
She javelins through and enters the river,
having ridden the spate for sixteen miles
in less than half a night. No weirs on her rivers,
nor Archimedes Screw, men with fyke or wing nets.
Darkness and spate keep the herons from hunting;
pike beat their gills in the shelter of tributary streams.
The only hazards collision and stranding.

Don racing with pallets and sundered
bankside trees. Unmoored narrowboat,
akimbo on the current. Stream lit
with invisible glitter; thousands of silver eels,
careering under Rawcliffe Bridge,
past the brimming drains of Decoy Farm,
to the swollen Ouse at the Port of Goole.
Broad river bellowed to the flat of its levees,
freighted with lumber and propane bottles,
loosed jetties and half-sunk cruisers.
Mute swans huge on the dark meniscus,
excited greylag, trumpeting overhead.
Eels from Derwent, Aire and Nidd,
the trickles of Peak, Dales, Wolds and Moors,
are carried downstream to the Danelaw's
vast collision of current: Trent Falls,
where tonnage of tumbling Mercian eels
join to form the swollen Humber's catadromous flow.
Spate pushes back the turning tide
from Whitton to Saltend Chemical Park,
where dawn breaks and the sea shoves back.

She sinks with the shoal in the silts of the P&O sea-lane,
and buries herself in the suction-dredged deep sands.

In estuarine gloom, tight in her tunnel
in the submarine muck, she braces herself
against the flood and calibrates her taxes.
Atlantic salt in procellariid nostrils
and her glass eel's imprinted geomagnetic memory
lay down her path before her. She pokes out her head
and waits for the tide to turn: Miocene gaze,
underslung hook-jaw, metronome billow of breathing.
The sonic assaults of the thundering Humber—
huge screws of the MV Olympic Legacy,
the diesel reverb of the Pride of Zeebrugge—
send shockwaves down her lateral line
and rattle the bones of her fine-tuned inner ear.
The back-flushed sewage of the Pride of Hull
settles its stink in the wormy silts around her.
Harbour seals rummage in the sunken filth,
plucking out shellfish, flounder and eel.
Shoals of predatory mullet and bass,
cormorants and divers attendant: the benthic ghost
of a twenty-five-foot sturgeon. Draws in her head,
hides in the dark till darkness.

Sucked out of her socket in the ebb-tide's gloom,
she sets her compass south past Spurn
and for six hours swims with the drag
of the seaward current. In the fifteen-fathom
bombing range offshore from Donna Nook,
the ebb-tide stalls and the flow turns back to Humber.
She sits out the flood in her seafloor sangar,
Thunderbolt autocannon ripping overhead,

torpedo shoals of arrowhead coley
exploding in the silts—from Silver Pit to Southern Bight,
the seabed's combed with the bivouacs of eels,
each one aimed blind in its Tomahawk head
for the hypertonic cauldron of Sargasso.
They labour tidal miles twice-daily,
a shallow-sea trudge to the race of the open Atlantic.
Some stumble in the water column
like warfarin-poisoned rats, swim bladders blown
by the *Anguillicola* nematode,
unable to make either current or anchor—
gulped down by shoals of cruising cod,
the baleen gapes of minkes. Skate and dogfish
take their tolls, the maws of white-beaked dolphins,
but only a week after leaving her cave
she's travelled the length of the Saxon Shore
to the undersea forest of turbine towers
at Vattenfall's Thanet Wind Farm.
Squeezed into a crack in the concrete foundation,
she breathes in capital's benzoylecgonine outflow,
the insufflated pisspots of Parliament and City:
hyperactivity, degeneration, cardiac distress.
Resisting infection and chemical assault,
she passes through the White Cliffs' garrisoned straits
into Lime Street's limitless, hyperactive
sea-lanes—renownèd, stubborn as Jewry.

I'm making it up as they go along.
Almost nothing demonstrated, almost
everything inferred. Once in the ocean,
they disappear completely: the odd accidental
in a fisherman's net, off Brittany, Brindisi;
tagged experimental fish, lost in the Waddenzee;

undigested, predated fish, cut from the guts
of Azorean cachalots and googly-eyed cod
longlined off Kilda. The leptocephalus data-sets
Schmidt produced from Dana's trawls
led to a certain hypothesis: eels spawn
in the depths of the southern Sargasso
and their highway to and from there
is the North Atlantic Gyre—where not a single
anguillid eel has ever been caught or seen.
'Somehow', then, along the Channel,
dragged limp on dark and ebbing tides—
or hard-gained miles in the pummelling face of flood.
Avoiding the light and its armies of killers
past Brighton and the Isle of Wight,
she snakes in the murk of the bottoms by day
and rises into the tidal race at night—
each phototaxic diurnal dive getting deeper
by the day, as English coasts decline
to broad Atlantic. Past Portland and Cotentin,
she swims above the seabed silts
in seventy or eighty fathoms of murk,
through the wreckage of Affray and Sala's Piper Malibu,
down the slope of the Biscay shelf
to the bottomless tohuwabohu of ocean.
Faint eel scent wafts along the channel
from the west; migrants from Baltic,
Rhineland and Gaul, ahead of her
on their journey. But there is no shoal,
no synchronous tonnage of travelling fish,
to be picked up on sonar and hoovered
into holds, like the sand-lance of Dogger,
or Madeiran sardines—she's making her own way,

one of ten, or five-hundred million, vanished
in the vastness of *oceanus incognitus*,
blind to the lung-tethered lubbers on land,
the white-coats and accountants of the inventoried seas.

Sometimes on her journey, eel scent surges,
and she senses along her lateral line
the congenial electricity of a fellow nuptial pilgrim.
For minutes, hours, or even days, until one lags,
or a marlin's intervention, she'll wind in time
with her dark companion, twin sextants set
for the distant warm salt sea. If she had eyes
designed to see, and not those supersized,
glaucous goggles, fit only to meter the lux
of the undersea light, she'd see her counter-shaded,
epipelagic self—black-backed, white-bellied,
long-finned like a winter puffin—a glint
in the squint of submarine darkness, occulted
in that world—but not to the scabbardfish
or bluefin tuna, grey seal or bottlenose dolphin,
zooming from the gloom along the widening Channel,
to the cliff of the Shamrock Canyon.
Here, in the three-mile plummet to the Biscay Abyssal,
seal and dolphin return to their harbours
and scabbardfish sink to their depths;
but the bluefin persist into open ocean,
harrowing the holocaust photocline with xiphius,
macrocephalus, savage architeuthis.

Heading south-west on her entorhinal compass,
she senses the Grand Banks' salts in suspension
and enters the deep, olfactory race
of the thermohaline Azores current—

the north-eastern curve of the North Atlantic Gyre,
her fast track to Sargasso. Fifteen, twenty,
twenty-five miles a day, over the Azorean Fracture Zone
and the rise of the Meteor Seamount.
Loose in the flow, swimming or steering,
under shoals of scad and bubble-net humpbacks,
she joins the southbound Canary current
between Desertas and La Palma,
over the northern Cape Verde Plain.
Loose in the flow, swimming or steering,
twenty-five, thirty, fifty miles a day,
across dark continents of plummeting water
where serpents vent from the smoking depths
of a seafloor white with shackled blacks
and the wrecks of harpooned whales.
High over the collateral wastes of Empire,
a cordon is forming in the breadth of the current—
six hundred miles wide, a quarter-mile deep
and fifteen hundred miles in length.
Unnumbered millions of travelling eels,
flickering in the heave like flecks of lint,
dim glimmers of the constellations
their eyes have never seen. Transatlantic 747s
soar blind skies above them; Seawolves prowl
the opaque depths below: they have ceased to exist
in our world. But in theirs she's getting closer
to the amniotic graveyard hieron—she can smell it
in the waters, sense it in the stars, feel it
in the needle of her geomagnetic cortex—
electrochemical calibrations, sparking in the dark.

Offshore from San Antão, the buffeting Trade Winds
shoulder the flow in a swerve across the ocean:
the North Equatorial Current, Atlantic's conveyor
to the dark Antilles, two-and-a-half thousand
blind sea miles at ten or thirty or fifty miles a day.
The cordon narrows in the curve of the current,
and there, between the fifteen/twenty latitude lines
at two hundred and fifty fathoms of depth,
she senses for the first time, her fellow-travelling,
deep-spaced shoal: an ultrasound cacophony
of directional undulations, nerves tingling in the skin;
mucus chemtrails, heavy with hormones,
flooding the cells with sex; the muscular push
and billow of breathing, sometimes swimming
beyond or beside her, intersecting electrical vectors,
charging her aura, driving her on.

She's heavy with three or four million eggs
now, her white-kid belly deep-keeled
from throat to vent. Posterity's vessel,
she's reducing herself to the seed of her species' future,
every non-essential body-part—eyes and bones,
digestive tract—recycling to gonads and roe.
She's close to exhaustion, her energies almost spent.
Eight months and six thousand fasting miles
on the self-immolatory, pelican fuel
of the flesh of her gourmet body.
She ropes on through the water that buoys her,
the current she rides upon, over the rise
of the Atlantic Ridge, where thermal vents
and magma plumes infuse the shivering water column
with the signature iron and magnesium taste
of the molten basalt mantle—her imprinted

larval hippocampus knows she's almost there.
In the drench of natal metals in suspension
she crosses into the Antillean Atlantic
in the last of her swimming strength,
encountering the heat and salinity fronts
that tell her, at last, she's arrived at the place
of her birth and programmed death:
the Subtropical Convergence Zone
of the southern Sargasso, 17 degrees north,
59 degrees west, two hundred and fifty miles
east of Anguilla, where the inside curve
of the gyring current tears at the edge
of the brooding Miocene waters.
She parks in the current at fifteen hundred feet
and begins her transformation.

Waning gibbous, 71% visible, stacked banks
of cumulonimbus. Black ocean humping
and breaking. Taiwanese canning ships,
upping their nets, heading for Leeward harbours.
Skeins of pelicans straggling over dissipating wakes.
Darkness in all directions: firefly twin-props
winking overhead, soft neon of turquoise myctophids,
dimming from the deeps—barracudina,
onychoteuthis, a blizzard of marine snow—
and under the photocline's abyssal blackness,
livid as knife scars, or threadworms
in the water, a herded raft of drifting eels,
scattered across the Convergence Zone
like buffalo, or passenger pigeon,
two or three every fifty or a hundred yards
for two hundred thousand cubic miles of ocean.

She travels in the Antillean flow at twenty
or thirty miles a day, drenched in the scent
of her gleaming congeners, in the rush
of her oestrogen-saturated blood.
Cachalots cruise and tarpon loom,
but all her attention is inward now,
as her DNA completes the reprogramming
of her body, transforming it into a breeding machine.
The remnant nanograms of skeletal calcium
and the adipose fats from the wastes of her muscles
dissolve in the blood and transport
to the oocytes, which swell red gold
and ripen, flushing the pleated kid of her belly,
pressing against her oviduct's tingling trapdoor.
Blood bulges the loosening lips of her cloaca
and bruises the ventral fin red/blue.
She hangs in her depths like a Universe,
and waits to come into her Queendom.

A half-mile distant, a sixteen-inch male
is plundering his carcase to complete his transformation.
The remaining lipids of his glands and organs,
his muscular proteins and the minerals of his bones,
are transported to the testes and repurposed
to spermatogenesis, shoaling his belly with milt.
His silver eel livery blackens to carbon steel;
a finger-thin stripe from throat to vent
is all that remains of his wintry guillemot belly.
Blood-red speckling, vasodilation,
scarlet ventral and caudal fins. Hooked kype
like an upstream salmon. Blood banging
in the brain. He travels the towering
mesopelagic, searching in the darkness.

She's travelling west-by-north with the current,
a curve offshore from Windward.
Swollen like a pomegranate, her roseate coelom
thick with eggs, each microscopic seed
of blood lit in its aril of vitelline gold.
She winds in the flow like a length of fraying halyard,
the edge of coming apart. He's swimming
a hundred yards behind her, locked on
to her oestrogen contrail. They drift for days
on the whelming current, moving deeper
into the fabled sea: 19 degrees north, 61 west,
approaching the rise of the Puerto Rico Trench,
a hundred miles north of Barbuda.
Blue-blackness above; black-blackness below:
waning crescent, 24% visible, faint glow
of Deep Scattering's bioluminescence.
Diesel growl of longliners, trolling snoods
for snapper. Humpback and pilot whales,
wahoo and marlin, picking off the bounty—
a continent of eels coming into fruition
as far as fancy's lightless eye can see:
tiny males, rubberised veterans
of the hemispheric journey, hanging limp
in the drift like branches of flaccid sargassum,
completing their nuptial transformations;
others, already come into their ripeness,
are riding the pheromone bow-waves of females,
girthy as pythons, four or five feet long.
Soft explosions of pluming milt
flare from mesopelagic darkness,
as all around them, eels entwine
and jettison their loads. The water stinks of sex

and death—progesterone, testosterone,
ichthyotoxic blood. She shivers in the warm,
aphrodisiac current, every nerve-end tingling,
each tender tip engorged. He's drifting in her orbit now,
homed in on her cloacal trail. He loops
his snaky electron around her: she recoils,
and snaps her gaping, rat-trap jaw—not ready.
So, for the moment they simply swim together,
the nineteen-inch female, her underslung bicep of belly,
and her swollen bootlace suitor. They drift
with the current deep into black Sargasso.

20 degrees north, 62 west.
The outer rise of the Puerto Rico Trench,
a hundred miles north of Anguilla.
New Moon, 1% visible. Kraken darkness,
lit only by octopus phosphorescence
and the bright detonations of ejaculating eels.
They've been travelling in tandem for five days now,
through frittering flames of fertilised ova
and the disarticulate, space-junk fall
of dead and dying eels. This is their predestiny,
their inescapable fate, the fate of every Atlantic eel
since the Yucatán asteroid dropped its apocalypse
sixty-six million years ago—to ruin themselves
in the act of breeding and die in the dopamine afterglow,
drifting down from the towering heights of ocean
to the black red clays of the five-mile abyss,
layer upon layer upon googolplexian layer.
Their bodies are coming apart, held together
only by shrink-wrapped skin and the kamikaze
cerebellum that tells them *live!*—to breed and die.

They're running on neurosteroids now,
their muscular strength exhausted—it's now
or never. But her biochemical transformation
is finally complete—the dark-moon shudders
in her teleost womb and she's suddenly wreathed in sex.
He stiffens and begins his dance around her,
nosing the waters, advancing and retreating
in a tentative submarine hokey-cokey;
like he's scared to get close, like he's got
at least one glaucous eye on that gaping, rat-trap jaw.
She drifts and ignores him, gaping and closing
that rat-trap jaw, beckoning him forward,
until he finally plucks up the courage to touch,
coming under and rubbing her pulsing belly
with the nacelles of his head. He kneads the flesh
of her underbody with a zig-zag massage
from pleated throat to vent. She gapes and twitches, swims,
and for a while they move touch-tight together,
him coiling his cable around the rope of her body,
constricting and releasing, bringing her to the edge.
She gapes and twitches, apparently impassive—
but a landslide has started inside her.
He uncurls his coils and once more swims beneath her,
nuzzling at her leaking vent like a Typhoon
fuelling from a stratotanker, butting the bulge
of her loosening roe sac, triggering the sensory overload
that will release them both into the ecstasy of body,
the DMT and oxytocin rush of coitus and extinction.
Milt pumps down the tube of his urethra
and backs up at the sphincter of the vent;
he stiffens and ejaculates a depth charge
blast of sperm. She shivers and her gold load slides.

They couple in the milt cloud, lit in the shock
of its bloom—once more he's frotting the flange
of her vent and butting the walls of her coelom,
once more he ejaculates—again, and again—
until the hypertonic waters are smoking
with milt, and her shuddering body
can hold it back no longer. She cracks like a whip
and her body convulses, spurting gusher
after gusher of glittering golden ova,
sparks from the cornucopian flame
of Archaea's unkillable, dark pleroma,
quickening through the mist of sperm and rising
through the photocline to join the thermonuclear
microplankton of the drifting epipelagic.

/ˈiːlaɪ/

Infangtheof

Infangtheof—the right of the Parish
to hang and expropriate thieves.
Prebendary lining his pockets,
gift of the pork-barrel Minster,
courtesy of Úlfr, Knútr's liegeman,
who placed his scylfe on Cynesige's plate
in memory of Gunnwårar, his wife:
VLF LET AROERAN CYRICE
FOR HANVM & FOR GVWARA SAVLA.
Aldbrough—Állburh-on-Lambwath;
Ulleskelf—Úlfr's-scylfe, Állscylfe.
Disappeared en route to Jerusalem,
somewhere along le Chemin des Anglois.

Cynesige, Ealdred—Guillaume le Bâtard.
Thirteen carucates less an oxgang,
two thousand and sixty acres.
Sokemen, villans, bordars, slaves;
meadow, pasture, ings and church.
Tonsured runt from Rouen or the Ridings,
his eye on our chattels and fish-traps:
frames and fit-ups, asset-seizures—
long dogs, dip nets, Troopers.
Must be nice to own the cops, say the Squires
and Shilletos, Londesboroughs,
the York & Ainsty foxhounds.

Gallows, location unknown. The clear-
felled sacred grove on Church Street?
The bulldozed henge at Manor Garth?

The 'Keep Out' signs at Intake Farm,
the Leeds & District ASA?
Wolves hanging from the boughs
of the death-tree. In the dark of the moon
they loosen their lariats and fall into earth
and its waters. Slimy garottids,
mucus nooses, bronze-eyed
bankside stranglers. Boggarts
in the Ozendyke lowering lead coffins,
dropping their Arlesey bombs.

Inglnz Dreamin

Saturday, 18th of June, 1977.
After the nine-day trip to Austria,
six of them on the coach—Ostend, Heidelberg,
Achenkirch; God Save the Queen on the London
tower block; Tartan Bitter at the back
of Allied Supplies; Boysy 6 Hemsworth
Wanderers 2—or maybe that was the year
before, Saturday 19th?
                        Packed platform
at Moorthorpe, 6.25 to Ulle. Club trip
carnival atmosphere—dads n lads, gangs of kids,
one or two old blokes. Kids fucking about,
chasing through the waiting room—coal fire,
arse-polished, dark-wood benches. Station master
in gold-rimmed glasses, British Rail blues,
red piping—*I won't tell you again.* Plywood boxes
with cushioned seats. Sandwiches and tartan flasks
pulled from grubby ex-Army knapsacks.
Rods in sleeves and plastic tubes akimbo.
Green mesh of keep and landing nets,
three-month-old dried slime.
                              Dramatis personae,
the Wimpey boys: me, Wack, Georgie,
one or two Toshes—bed-hair, worn-out
Adidas Kick. And the big lads, almost
misters: Coco, Spanner, Scoffer or Doc—
Markham kohl and hacking Park Drive.
Loud ticks of the bright-faced station clock.
Shit-bed yawns and stretches.

                              The Whitsun Weddings
train pulls in. Tackle stashed in the filthy Baggage.
Lads sprawled among it, keeping an eye
on their stuff. Pop & crisps and fucking about:
Tosh—would you bum Buddy Holly? Dead-arms
and crowpecks. *Ow!*
                    Pontefract Baghill.
Sherburn-in-Elmet. RAF Church Fenton.
Finally, Ulle. Acre of exposed concrete platform,
wrought-iron steps to Main Street. Queuing
for day-tickets, back door of the brayed-up
Village Inn. Shoulder-strapped waddle
across the cowfield to the storied pegs
by the railway bridge. Spanner's derision—
nowt but flatties an bootlaces theer;
big barbel r up ont bend neart Ship.
Tosh, sotto voce—*barbel? Moor chance*
a catchin a dose. Spanner flashing white eyes,
dropping his plywood box. *What did tha seh,*
y cheeky lickle cunt? Tosh, bug-eyed rabbit
in the beam. Wack stepping up, courage
of his borstal brothers—*leave im Mark,*
e dint mean owt. Coco settling it down,
common-sense authority, Victor Mature—
leave im Mark, e's not wuth it—we've got t
get t pegs, befoor sumbdy else digs in.
   Georgie set me up, opposite the ivied ruin
on the Bolton Percy side. Lappies and skylarks,
bubbling curlew, swallows flicking underneath
the arches of the bridge. His second-best rod,
his second-best reel; Arlesey bomb rig,
six-pound line. Brandling from the gravels

of the trickling filter. I cast and tightened,
waited. Waited. The others were reeling them in:
Wack whipping flatties from under the bridge,
Georgie landing a glittering dace, Tosh,
a fighting, two-pound chub. He credited
his new reel—a spinner with a bail arm.
I landed slime, then snapped the line on weed.
Georgie said he'd sort me out, but he was messing
with his rig. I got sick of waiting
and took off nesting: four-egger swallow
crusted under the arches; colony of spuggies
in the ruinous ivy; twenty-egger part,
deep in the Yorkshire Fog.
                                    I was gone half-an-hour
and missed everything: Wack had caught
a flatty the size of a dustbin lid. Tosh had lost
a pike that nearly took his hand off.
Georgie had knocked his box into the swim,
and had to crawl like Spitz to retrieve it.
And Spanner had borrowed Tosh's reel,
despite his roorin protestations—*please Mark,*
dunt tek it, it's new; mi Dad sez av not got t
borrer it nobdy. Spanner shaking his head
and shoving him aside—*I've asked thi nice,*
na tha's got no choice.
                           Georgie set me up—
second-best rod, second-best reel, two Swan
on six-pound line. I dropped it short of the far bank,
in the deep, clear swim I'd been missing
all morning. *At last,* he said. *Art a that fuckin weed.*
The line twitched. The rod-tip bent. I struck
and started to reel. Something broke the water—

a flash of thumb-thick, twisting cable,
spasming on the line—*bootlace!*
Georgie rushed round with the landing net,
but I swung it to the bank on the six-pound braid
and rummaged in the box for the forceps.
Y can't disgorge em, Georgie said.
They tek it too deep. Y've got to chop their eads off!
Forceps in the right hand, eel squirming in the left,
a flex of greasy liquorice. I couldn't get a grip,
juggling and reeling on the sloping bankside,
almost tippling in—*kill it befoor thy ends up int river!*
It's not your fuckin tackle!
                              I didn't want to kill it.
I didn't want to kill anything. And I thought,
perhaps if I furtively cut the line,
I could pretend that the eel had somehow
snapped it, and allow it to slither away.
My tackle-less ineptitude would be the perfect alibi.
So, with Georgie looking down from the top
of the bank, I pinned it to the muck with the heel
of my palm and took out my penknife.
Pitiful bronze-eyed gaze and gape, desperate,
pathetic—*chop its fuckin ead off!* As I fumbled
to cut the line, it slipped my grip and—*JESUS CHRIST!*
IT BIT ME! The barb of a hook, or the jolt
from an electric fence, between the mount of Venus
and the plain of Mars, on the lifeline
where the nails drive in. And the blood
came forth—*CHOP ITS FUCKIN EAD OFF!*
I seized it with the grip of my cuff and wedged it
against a stone—pitiful bronze-eyed gaze
and gape, desperate, pathetic—and sawed through

the slimy, newt-green skin until the rubbery
snake-length severed. I pulled out the hook—
heart and liver, ropes of beige intestine.
Decapitated, eviscerated, its eely life
had not yet left it, gills working air and torn mouth
gaping, convulsing into the bankside nettlebed—
down the neck of Tosh's t-shirt.
                                    On the train home,
Tosh got his reel back, and a gut-punch
for being a mawngy cunt. We straightened out
our fishermen's tales, all but mine a record.
My eel-bite failed to convince—hook-tear,
slippery penknife. The first cut is the deepest.

Dads at Lads

Ron was summat at Harvesters. Paid-up
on account of his knee. Drove us to football
in his immaculate yellow Cortina.
Black vinyl roof, polar bear seat covers.
    Oi! Get thi feet off them covers.
    Shut it Fatha, tha showin me up.
    I'll gi thi shut it, y cheeky little beggar.
    Ar, coorse tha will.
    Tha'll see.
    Ar, when eyes r poork pies.
Stan worked at Kirkby, double-uns,
weekends, neets. Tinnitus? Tired. Joey
the Budgie.
    Dave drove a reach-truck
at Birds Eye. Walked out the gates
with a salmon down his knackers.
Euclid at the oppen-cast. Zebra finch.
Amway. Club turn? *Scut.* Car-full to Ulle
in his black Cortina—window sticker:
I Like Knockers.
    Jim walking through the ginnel
with his staffies. *Oreyt cock.*
Brandy and Lady. Duck's Arse,
Khaki Campbells.
    Clarrie with his tache
and blue Cortina, FBE 903L. Foorman
at Frigo. Football n cricket, Satdy n Sundy,
Kirkby n Upton, Jube. Totes n sweeps.
Albatross, *Sailing*. Fishing is boring.
Adidas, Puma—no tackle.

The Leeds & District ASA

WMC Crawl

The Diamond Jubilee, followed by the Coronation.
On to the Empire, past the tent city on Donkey Lane,
finishing at the Pretoria. A good crowd,
all the right people, Vickie, Bertie, Winnie, Fred.
[Sir] John Austin. [Sir] Joseph [Compton-]Rickett.
[Sir] H.H. Campbell[-Bannerman]. God save
& God bless. In their cups, it got a little out of hand.
Some bother with the forces of disorder,
the black figures of famine, pestilence and crime.
Herbert Smith in his flat cap and dicky-bow:
leave it—you're better than that! The Divisions
of the State: magistrates, bayonets, tit-heads
& taprooms. The watch-chains and Homburgs
of the Rural District Council. It got sorted in the end—
somehow we always muddle through. Last orders
in the committee room: Bollinger, Courvoisier, Boodles,
Glenlivet. And a round for the tap: Spartacists, blacklegs,
the Osgoldcross militia—stout, mild and bitter.

Any Other Business

Mr. Thoroldsson proposed that non-members should be banned from fishing the Society's soke on the Wharfe, pegs 1-100, from the Railway Bridge to the Ship, including pegs 1-25, currently reserved for day-ticket pleasure anglers on Saturdays in season only, on account that strangers killed his calf with idlebacks. Seconded by *Mr. Londesborough*, passed unanimously. Ban imposed with immediate effect. *Mr. Shilleto* said that strangers would come anyway, by car and train, and fish at night. They have frequently shoplifted in the Post Office. *Mr. Thoroldsson* proposed that bailiffs be posted on the platform with orders to turn them back, and that the station platform be circled with electrified wire. *Mrs. Lumb* proposed that roadblocks be set at the entry points to the parish, where papers might be checked and entry refused to those with certain kinds of faces. *Chief Superintendent Squire* seconded both proposals, which were passed unanimously. *C.S. Squire* to ensure the measures are implemented without delay. *Captain Fielden* from the chair brought it to the meeting's attention that he had been introduced to the celebrated broadcaster and charity worker, Sir James Wilson Vincent Savile, O.B.E., K.C.S.G., at Peter Corrigan's arcade in Scarborough, and that Sir James had agreed, subject to the meeting's approval, to become Honorary Life-President of the Society, and, once in place, would be willing to deejay at a fundraising event for the Society, to be held at the Ship. *Mrs. Lumb* was agreeable in principle, but as proprietor and licensee at the Ship, expressed her displeasure that she was not consulted about the proposed event before *Capt. Fielden* made his approach to Sir James, considering this a lack of basic courtesy. As a matter of information, she had already secured the services of Sir Adrian Juste to deejay at a charity 'barn dance' organised by the Lions, to be held at the Ship in August, and is concerned that the likely similarity of the two events might have the effect of depressing attendances at both, as well as posing the usual organisational challenges. *Capt. Fielden* apologised to *Mrs. Lumb* for any inadvertent discourtesy, but stressed he had been acting *ex officio* in the best interests of the Society. *Mrs. Lumb* asked *Capt. Fielden* if Sir James had indicated whether or not he would like to fish the river during his visit; Sir Adrian is Honorary Life-President of the Royal British & Commonwealth Sodality of the Barbel, and part of the agreement with him is, that on the Saturday of the 'barn dance', he might, as an Honoured Guest, fish the renowned 'peg 88' below the rapids, free of charge or necessity of ticket. *Capt. Fielden* was not aware if Sir James was an angler or not, but thought, as a courtesy and in the interests of equity, that a similar invitation ought to be extended to him. *Mr. Thoroldsson* proposed that Sir James be invited to become Honorary Life-President of the Society and that both Sir James and Sir Adrian should be allowed to fish the river on any in-season dates, as Honoured Guests, free of charge or necessity of ticket, but not between dusk and dawn, or on match days. *Mr. Londesborough* seconded, and thanked *Capt. Fielden* on behalf of the meeting for securing such a great coup for the Society. The proposal was passed 11-0, with *Mrs. Lumb* abstaining. *Capt. Fielden* to liaise with Sir James, *C.S. Squire* and *Mrs. Lumb* to make the arrangements.

/ˈstiːvnz/ *Rod*

Take thy rod and cast it in Pharaoh's river,
in the presence of his bailiffs, policemen
and solicitors; where the maggots released
from the feeder shall be transformed into serpents,
devouring his salmons, trouts and barbels;
and which shall clamber the banks to swallow
his armies, the enchantments of Zaphnath-Paaneah.
Nehushtan aloft on the carbon-fibre pole,
a burning sign, and wonder. The stink-pits
swarm with fierie worms: under the skin,
in the rectal cavity, spilling from the sockets
of the eyes—bronze, pink and casters.

And there is fishing and access, no danger
to dogs, and all is strictly public. Whence
comest thou? From going to and fro
in the earth, and walking up and down in it.

The Barkstone Ash & Skyrac Volunteers

Níðhǫggr gnawing at the root of the Barkston Ash,
sidling up the hollow trunk, dangling
from the branches. *Look into my eyes.*
Nothing will be restrained from you
of which you can imagine. No apples,
only keys.
    Bee as Gods. Gascoigne of Parlington Hall,
braid, cockades and epaulettes, hunter,
cut-and-thrust sword. Rank and file:
slub, fuzee and bayonet. Shilling a day
for manoeuvres and musters. Beer-tap,
beef and cobblers.
    Be like God. Fitzwilliam,
Howard, 'the sovereign majesty of the people':
gamekeepers, grooms and ploughmen.
Grocers and locksmiths. Apples and keys.
John Reeves and Anton Drexler.
        Dragon-prowed
longships, riding Wharfe from Humber
and Bantry Bay. Ívarr, Hoche, Wolfe Tone.
The London Corresponding Society.
Enemies without and within. Beacons flaming
from Fishguard and Killala, Otmoor
and Ottiwells Mill.

                Flotillas of little boats,
chugging upriver to meet them, armed
to the teeth with little flags, choler and bile.
God save the King, his Constitution!
God save Old England and the UVF!
They beat up some incomers, antis and Pakis,
before the grandad eel sucked their brains.
Three cheers for Boris! Three cheers for the NHS!
    Níðhǫggr in the gallows of the hoary crabtree.
The Barkston Ash has fallen. No keys but Enoch's,
the dangling corpses of nightfishing Luddites
and ticketless Bolshevik miners. *Imagine.*
Crabs tart and bitter.

Gibbets

Predator Control

Johnson, Castlereagh, the Chief Exec
of Natural England. The Countryfile
Association. Rat-faced moochers in moleskin caps,
splenetic former corporals. Bully Beef.
Lord Snooty. Bodie, and possibly Doyle.
Unionists, UKIP, National Action.
Munitions and certificates, Glen Brown
and Alan Wilson. Sir & Ma'am, Your
Lordship. Foreskins tugged, ringpieces
expertly licked. London/The Country.

Vermin

Heron, cormorant, goosander, smew:
dabchick, black-necked grebe.
Butterbump. Kingfisher. Earn æftan hwit.
Dipper, pied wagtail: red-throated diver.
Lutra. Aigrettes, osprey, trana.
The harmless and disarming. The plucky,
seized and summonsed. Ben Rothman.
Alf Tupper and Dead Shot Keen.
Possibly Wolfie, almost certainly Shirl.
Lamprey, pike and burbot. Anguilla.

The Bridge

Why the Bridge? That's where you ended up.
Over the PRIVATE five-bar gate, across Dort's Dyke,
and tiptoe through the cowpats to the river.
The direct route. A walk along Main Street
took you to the snicket that led to the pegs
near the Ship, but you had to know that.
I thought the Ship was a ship. I imagined
it as a wreck in the river, prowled by pike
and eels the size of congers. Cut-throat lads
with love/hate knuckles. Best stay down
near the Bridge.
                    Red-brick abutments, span
of girdered steel, flood-relief arches stacked
with Wharfedale's washed-down sheep
and ripped-out bankside alders. Hirundine trifecta:
swallows under the arches; house martins
under the span; sand martins in the river cliff.
Good fishing under the Bridge, we told ourselves.
You could stand on the piles and spin for pike,
catch flatties on the feeder. Krakatoa thunder
when the trains went over, stones dropping
and plopping like the piers were coming down.
That's what we liked, the frisson, the risk—
stranded on the piles, surprised by the speed
of the turning tide, edging back to bankside,
starfished against the wall.
                              Nesting when nothing
was biting—under the arches, up onto the Bridge,
down the embankment on the Bolton Percy side:
Wood Hill Close, where labourers repairing

the flood-torn embankment found a hoard
of 4000 Northumbrian stycas—
'the monetary wealth of the township
or parish at the time of the Danish irruption'.
Not an Englishman left to recover it.
500 recovered for York Museum. The rest
disappeared into private hands by the Colonel's
antiquarian fences.
     Which we vaulted,
roaming the pastures, coverts and woods,
the lodge-lands by the river—jackdaw, curlew,
lapwing, doves—stranded aloft in the ivied ruin
by a herd of bellowing Holsteins,
shouldering the walls and rickety elders,
trying to shake us down. Sprint back
to the British Rail five-wire fence at the head
of the pied stampede. Driven back by jeering
barrage of ballast. Across the Bridge,
the slid embankment, freight train blaring
its horn.
    8th December, 1981. The 13.50
York to Liverpool train derailed on a broken
cess side rail exactly a yard to the south
of the bridge, exactly where we'd scramble
up and down. The two back carriages jumped
the track and decoupled down the east embankment
to settle among the pats. One dead,
twenty-three in the infirmary. We were sitting
on our boxes, backs turned against the roar,
from New Rose to Dead Cities. Peroxide
and painted biker-jackets, X-Clothes,
Abu Garcia. Her Majesty's Inspector of Railways,

Lieutenant-Colonel A.G. Thompson-Rose,
late of the Royal Engineers, ruled out
vandalism. The evidence suggested
a fracture in the weld and inadequately
ballast-tamped way-beams.
                                I don't believe
I was thinking of eels in December 81—
Luteros! for the People. Me and eels
were probably done by then. Five or six
fishing trips to Ulle. At least one bootlace.
Nowt else I can remember. The bite.

Plum

Late November, Ulleskelf station,
early evening darkness. Fog rolling
up the river from the German Sea.
The hiss of gas, a flickering candle;
figures, indistinct: a man on a bench,
reading an opened newspaper; a boy
with a stick or fishing rod; liveried
official of the North-Eastern Railway,
hurrying down the platform. Empty
coal train on the up-Leeds line, waiting
for the signal. The up-Normanton
rail begins to sing. Shrill whistle,
earthquake rumble, thundering billow
of sulphur and steam. Diminuendo
down the track, a momentary robin:
a bomb explodes, the coal-trucks
clatter, the screech of shearing metal—

Lieutenant-Colonel Pelham George
von Donop, Inspector of Railways,
Board of Trade. Formerly of the Royal
Engineers. The York-to-Leeds express,
running nine minutes late, ran into
the back of a waiting coal train,
headed for Gascoigne Wood.
Statements taken: signalmen,
drivers, firemen, guards. Wilkinson,
the station master. Scrutiny of wreckage
and infrastructure—rolling stock,
signals, permanent way. Enquiries

at the North-Eastern, the characters
of the deceased; fireman Booth
and driver Dunham—teetotal,
exemplary—but who had nevertheless
driven through signals 'on danger',
presumably blinded, not by the fog,
which was not particularly dense,
but by the smoke and steam
of the Manchester express,
running parallel and just ahead.

F.A. Cup finals, 74 & 75, v.
Oxford and Old Etonians. Capped
twice for England, both times v.
the Scots. Wimbledon singles, 82.
91 not out v. Quins. Nile Expedition,
Bombay Gymkhana. Marriage
to Ethel reported in John Bull—
10th of May, 1890. Left the Sappers
for the Inspectorate, 1899. Promoted,
Chief Inspecting Officer, July 1913.
One hundred and eighty-two reports:
mettle, fatigue, systemic and human
error—how many dead fellahs
between Sarras and Akasha,
dead weavers in the plague-pits
of Girangaon? It wasn't his fault.
Godfather, Jeeves and Wooster.

The Ship

… horrible 80s disco pub, purple,
mirrors, carpets. Ambient bleeps
from fruit machines, Matsui
television. Sliding doors, lawns
sloping to the river. First and only visit—
spring Satdy dinner, sometime
between 1995 and *maybe* 2003.
Can't pin it down. Completely empty.
Me, Tosh—barman? Long-time no-see,
bankside walk, nostalgic nesting,
bar-meal, pint …

… barman? landlord, local. Wayne.
Clive. *Gary.* Permatan swinger,
blond streaks, black wet-look t-shirt.
Regal King Size, white crocodile
loafers, curb chains/Cuban links.
Not from round here—fishing?
I think I told him birdwatching.
Birdwatching? Did he just imply
we were gay? Did he actually
accuse us of bumming in the bushes?
Did he actually say, get back
to where you come from, cunts,
with your bumming fucking rucksacks
and binoculars? …

… we should have dropped him
where he stood. If it happened like that.
Even if it didn't. Did we really just look
at each other like twats and take it?
*Ignore him, we're bigger than that:
what an oaf!*—Next time we'll come
down the Wharfe in longships,
and blood eagle *Gary* on the purple
baize of his American Standard table—

… *long-time-no-see*. The occasion—
after me Dad died, after the floods,
after you'd returned from away?
Nesting would've been my idea.
You'd not been bothered for yonks,
and seemed faintly embarrassed
by my lack of progression.
I wanted to relive 81, the curlews,
doves and jackdaws—*get a young un
and rear it up!* …

… 9.29am, Moorthorpe Station,
Thursday 28th March, 2002. The ghosts
of von Donop and Thompson-Rose,
the verdict of David Hinchliffe—
Total Body Disruption. Long ticks
of the absent station clock.
Venlafaxine blur. Spreadsheets
blowing down the permanent way.
Fluttering crime-scene tape.
Bouquet of smashed carnations.
Blood-spatter across the ballast.
Worse—

… Flood tourism with Elliot,
October 01 [03, 05, 07?]. Everything's
a senile blur. Don, Dearne, Went—
Wharfe. Scrambling over the five-bar gate,
the anti-climactic, cow-pat field.
Never mind, first one to the river
up the flood-bank! and
WHOA! My knees actually went!—
river on the point of bellying over,
a hundred turbulent yards across,
five times its usual breadth—windmilling
backwards to keep from toppling in.
A pair of mergansers, diving
among the horseboxes,
Harewood's swept-down flotsam …

… Adrian Juste on Donkey Kong,
going for Jimmy's hi-score. Su Pollard
in leather trousers and Su Pollard glasses.
Malandra Burrows karaoke,
'Just this Side of Love'. Minders
and agents prowling. Boycott in linen
and Panama hat, t-shirt printed
with an image of himself—*Legend*.
Him off Calendar with the ferret.
Gammon-faced farmers-cum-
haulage contractors, in dealers
and Tattershall shirts. Long ticks
of the bright-faced Acctim clock.
Silver eels fleeing downstream …

John's & Sam's

Two brothers, Ad and Rude olf
Dassler. Best götzendämmerung
training shoes in the whole
of the Teutoburg Forest, as worn
by Owens and Luz—*oh, the brown
and the yellow ale!* Hide Hickler!
de Nazification, de fraternization,
de rise of FIFA and de IOC.
Canaan able, Puma, La Marque
Aux 3 Bandes. King—Pele, Cruyff,
Maradona. Copas—Franz, Michel,
Zizou. In a twist of fate, the estranged
brüders were reunited in death,
crashing head-on in their near-identical
custom bugs at the Oberammergau
Oktoberfest, 19 hundred and 80.
Adi on John's, Rudi on Sam's,
blood alcohol durch das dach.
They were buried at sea off Danzig,
where their skulls were sucked
by vampire anguillids, which had entered
the Baltic some years previously,
having journeyed from Sargasso,
where their sire was a bootlace
from Ulle on the Wharfe, two miles
downstream from the factories
that cooked the suds that killed them.

[The eels were killed and served
with spätzle to their beautiful
virgin daughters, putting them
die Ente hoch. In six, or nine,
or eighteen months, each one
gave birth to a nameless thing
the peasants demanded be sealed
in das stattliches wohnhaus walls.
Where they remain *to this day*,
crawling through the cracks
in the crumbling mortar to tongue
the tingling air, brooding
on their inheritance.]

/ˈstiːvn/

Jimmy Deadbait

The bridge at Ulle, man fishing
with a clothesline. Neither float, nor box,
or landing net. A hessian sack
beside him, and another under his arse.

/ˈstiːvn/ hallooed him, and asked him
what? etc. Face of a rat in a greasy flat cap,
rat tails to the collar of his filthy
Tattershall shirt. Grin like a piano keyboard.

I watched as he hauled it in, the slash
of tensile water, buntings of khaki slime.
/ˈstiːvn/ craned closer, and watched as a pair
of luminous buttocks broke the dirty water.

Gaffed to the bank through the sockets
of the eyes—an emaciated, lard-white
gimmer, ribbed like the South Bay sands.
Peroxide mullet, gold lamé shell-suit.

/ˈstiːvn/ could not believe it.
Face of a rat in a greasy flat cap,
grin like a piano keyboard—*I dug the bastard up!*
Full beam Michael Fabricant.

He reached into the ribcage, scooped out
a fistful of little green eels and put them
into his sack. /ˈstiːvn/ reared away
and retched. Jesus Christ! The stench!

Grin like a piano keyboard—*worse than a dead cat!*
Full beam Michael Fabricant. Two turd-brown
eels, one prised from each socket, plus one
from the ear, a mess of dribbling cottage cheese.

/ˈstiːvn/ slid down the bank on his vomit.
There he goes!—full beam Michael Fabricant.
He had his arm up the dead man's arse
to the elbow, like he was groping for a calf.

The sphincter popped like a champagne cork.
The man flew back in a shower of shit,
gripping an eel the size of a pet shop python.
Grin like a rack of chisels. Whistling Peter Sutcliffe.

The Serenade of the Black Dwarfs

I landed a burbot from under the Bridge.
Don't kill me, he begged. *I am the last
of my kind.* He was a talking burbot
from a fairytale, a prince or fishy king.
And he said, *Please, good sir, return me
to the river. In gratitude, I will grant
to thee thy dearest human wish.* I would have
put him back anyway—I had a keep net
for God's sake. But /ˈstiːvn/, as ever,
was keen to scry in his future's dark palantir.
The burbot gasped his maimed consent,
so I carefully disgorged him, and lowered
him into Wharfe. At that moment, thirteen
black dwarfs appeared on the Bolton Percy side.
They adjusted their saxophones and began

their serenade. *Everyone you love will die
and you will masturbate as they are dying.*
The song went on until the sun exploded
over the Land of Nod. And I murmured
to myself, is there nothing I can do? For I had seen
the little diggers making trenches in the fen,
the gibbets in the rafters of the attic.
And /ˈstiːvn/ so loved the world, he wished
the burbot would strike him dead, that his life
might be accepted in the place of his belovèds.
But the burbot and his dwarfs had vanished,
leaving him with nothing but his eel in his hand.

Jimmy the Tiger

Me and Puttoc, top set Maths,
putting our band together. ~~Luteros
For The People! Luteros! for the People.
Luteros! for the people!~~ Trouble
with capitals and exclamations.
Classic punk line-up—drums & base,
guitar & vocals. Cook and Matlock,
Jones and Rotten—me and Puttoc.
Neither of us could sing or play
a note. Drums, piano, clarinet:
Krupa, Wilson, Goodman—a kick-line
of thirteen black dwarfs. Set list,
numbers: Missis Biddle plays the Fiddle;
Witch, Witch, Black as Pitch; the Blue Danube.
Compositions of our own: Acid Bath,
Arson, Crucifiction. Foxtrots, waltzes,
Pogo Patterson: bum-tit-tit, bum-tit-tit,

play your titty banjo. Savile: behave.
/ˈstiːvn/: fuck off, you lacquer-head nonce.
Principal's office, threats and cajoling:
what a waste, you could be—*the sergeant
in a squadron full of wallahs?*—Oxford!
PPE! La crème de la crème!—Absolute
refusal to apologise, but somehow back
at the back with Puttoc. Mine o' Serpents,
Do the Worm and Maggot. Jesus is Cool.
Flicking spitballs, jean-ripping drum-roll farting:
Patricia looking daggers: *Oh, grow up!*
14% on the mock exam. Puttoc only 10.
How on earth did we get away with it?
Savile with his hand up Barbara's skirt.
Savile with his hands in Teresa's d-cups.
Patricia with her fist in Savile's opened flies,
shunted up the back wall of his stockroom.

/ˈstiːvn ˈiːlaɪ/ *is a puff*

I had it all worked out. Or a kind of vague idea.
I'd read books and go nesting. Play football
with my mates. Hopefully lose my virginity.
Write books when I grew up or got round to it:
the Robin Reliant went phut-phut-phut;
the rude dude had a crude attitude to the nude;
a quicksilver flash of trout. *A bizarre tale, B+.*
Then go work for David Attenborough.
But /ˈstiːvn/ handed me a pale, forked root.
See this? he said. It's heroin and LSD.
I grow it in the garden. Long, deep pots,
ex-chymbley. I took a bite, and my books

were nests, and all my nests were books.
I woke beneath a hawthorn hedge, rough tongue
of a Friesian cow. I blinked it into /ˈstiːvn/.
He handed me a pair of pointy shoes.
See these? he said. They're winklepickers.
I wear them on Top of the Pops. I put them on—
and I was on the bench, and the colored girls
called me gay. I came round by the five-bar gate,
the rubbery lips and rasping licks of a mouthy
Friesian cow. I blinked and it was /ˈstiːvn/.
He handed me an M16. See this? he said.
It's what I use to rule the world, after the nukes
have tumbled down. Words failed me.
David Attenborough's assistant sent me
a kind rejection. And I surfaced on the banks
of the Wharfe at Ulle in a radioactive hecatomb
of discotheque Friesians and foul-hooked bootlace eels.
And Babs and Trish and the colored girls go,
do-do-do, do-do, do-do, do-do-do do, do-do, do-
do—/ˈstiːvn ˈiːlaɪ/ is a puff, doo-dah, doo-dah,
/ˈstiːvn ˈiːlaɪ/ is a puff, doo-dah, doo-dah, day.

Jörmungandr

Lightweight Thor, struggling to finish
his pint, outwrestled by the cat. Off fishing
with Hymir for flatties and sperm whales.
Hymir picking brandlings from the trickling filter.
Thor lopping an ox-head in the cow-pat field.
They lowered their rods in the abyssopelagic,
opposite peg 88. Hymir, bored, nowt biting.
Thor looks across, excited—feels like he's got

summat on. Churning water, biceps straining,
rod bending like a paperclip—out comes
the grandad eel, spitting venom and ichthyotoxic
blood. World coming apart at its distant edges.
Thor dragging him up the bank. Seas falling
from the world-cliff into space. Thor raising
brutal Mjǫllnir. Bridge toppling into the river.
Thor bringing down the batterer—piss-taking
Hymir cuts the six-pound line. Jörmungandr
coils to his tumbling depths, and the earth stops
shaking: Hymir stroking his cat like Blofeld.
Thor jumping on his hat with bloody feet.
His day will come, when he'll hoist out
the Earth-Girdler from the pond by Carr Side Farm
and bray in his head with the hammer.
Middle-Earth quaking to wreckage around him.
Rivers boiling off to Hel. The walls of the borstals
tumbling down, releasing Wolfie, Spanner
and Puttoc, /ˈstiːvn ˈiːlaɪ/, the bairns of Loki.

marvelous weraal origin story

[it's a great day for fishing on the wharfe] *maybe i can break my duck and finally catch a fish!* [but things don't go to plan] *damn! that's the third time my line's snapped on this weed* [the blind moon rises] *a final cast, then i'll have to go for the last train home* [the rod tip bends] *a bite!* [/ˈstiːvn/ plays the fish] *feels like a whopper! maybe i've hooked the grandad pike!* [but when the fish breaks the water, /ˈstiːvn/ is disappointed] *oh no! it's just a bootlace!* [he swings the eel bankside] *look at it knotting and twisting on the hook, like a shock of greasy volt*

age! it's going to take some disgorging!* [/ˈstiːvn/ at
tempts to disgorge the eel, but the slimy snake-fish wrig
gles from his grip] *damn it! i'll use the cuff of my jum
per to get a firm hold!* [/ˈstiːvn/ finally pins the
writhing bootlace] *now to cut off its head—it might sound
cruel, but it's the only way to disgorge them. they
take the bait too deep!* [but as /ˈstiːvn/ unfolds his pen
knife, his glance locks on to the eyes of the eel] *those pit
iful bronze eyes ... a gaze from the depths of the olig
ocene tethys ... i can't do it!* [the eel stares unblink
ing] *i'll cut the line and release him* [the eel begins
to squirm in /ˈstiːvn's/ grip] *stay still, damn you! i'm trying
to save your life!* [/ˈstiːvn/ lowers the blade to cut the
six-pound line] *stop wriggling!* [the bootlace slithers from /ˈsti
ːvn's/ grip] *for god's sake! do you actually want to die?*
[/ˈstiːvn/ pins the little anaconda with the palm

of his left hand] *OW! it bit me!* [blood wells from /ˈstiːvn's/
lifeline] *that hurt! like a wasp sting, or the jolt from an
electric fence! i can feel the ichthyotoxines
burning!* [/ˈstiːvn's/ face contorts with rage] *so that's the way
you want to play it? well, two can play that game—take THIS!*
[/ˈstiːvn/ saws off the eel's fanged head and tosses it in
to the river] [he stares at the blood, welling from the
lifeline of his palm] [he raises his palm] [he licks it]
something feels ... strange ... something feels ... diffrent ...
            [/ˈstiːvn/ looks in
the river and gasps at his oily reflection] *bronze
eyes ... hook-jaw ... kneading pectorals ... i'm turning into ...
AN EEL!—from this day forward—*[/ˈstiːvn/ collapsed to a
coil on the slipry bankside and slid into the flow]

The American Mink

Shut railway tunnel for mushrooms,
spare brick shed for mink. Diversification
before it was a word. Sub-arctic carnivores
stacked in batteries and fed on meal. Ten or a dozen
big hobs will service fifty or even a hundred jills.
Five kits per litter on average: two hundred
and fifty, five hundred per annum. Up to a tenner
per pelt. Do the maths.
                    Plop. There goes the water vole.
Plop. There go the ditch and streamside nesting
moorhens. Plop, plop, plopetty-plop, kingfishers,
sand martins, sandpipers, dippers.
                            Fishing the Went
in a bower of hogweed, mesh of gnats
and scribbling midges. Wet-my-lips
in the wheatfield; from the hawthorns,
a-little-bit-of-bread-and-no-cheese.
The fish are not biting. Mink up and down
the opposite bank all day—escapees from the shed
on Rigg Lane, not the antis or the animal rights.
Bullfinch, linnet, the ghostly purr of a turtle dove.
Puits tumbling over the cow field.
                            Cow field for horses,
hawthorns for flailing and suburban sitting-room
woodstoves. Woodland 4x4 and paintball.
The acrid scent of glyphosate and Vera Lynn's
Agent Orange. Sheds for Tesco & B&Q,
cattle, pigs and chickens. Cow field for Barrett,
Persimmon and Wimpey.

            Interglacial omnivores,
stacked in batteries, fed on meals. A big hob
will service at least one jill, sometimes three or four.
Two-and-a-bit per litter, on average.
                              Do the maths.

Bollwurz

Maisbeli
488

Hengist in chains before Kaerconan.
Braids plastered across his forehead,
giblets matted in the elflocks of his beard.
Circle of gloating wealas, jabbing
swords and provocations. The old grey bear,
at bay in his pelt of blood and muck.
Noble Aurelius—surely the bitternesse
of death is past? The bishop demurred.
And Eldol hewed Hengist in pieces
before the high crag of Kaerconan.

Hengist roaming from his barrow
in the bungalow back garden, stitched-up
by wights from the Neolithic and Mexborough
Business Centre. Stonehenge, hengestán,
Hangmanstone Lane. Betrothed, of course,
to the Lady of the Well, the flooded
workings of Cadeby Main. Rain filters
through the limestone. Blood percolates from the Ings.
The snake-holes ooze rubies, black diamonds.
We crawl in our dust like worms.

Idlæ

616

Rædwald's powerplay in the waning moon
of Wotan. Æthelberht bretwalda
under Christ's sod, fingernails black with bollwurz;
Eadbald, Cynegils and Cearl subdued.
Trouble beyond the Northern Fen: Æthelfrith,
Ceretic, son of Gwallog. Rendlæsham,
Ermine Street, Lindum. 28a to the ings
by the burh at Scaftworth-on-Idle,
where the river ran foul with English blood:
Edwin, Rædwald's king beyond Humber.

The pike fed well, and Rendlæsham's sturgeon,
migrating up the Idle to their redds
in the gravels of the Poulter. The king lopped
the river like Cromwell lopped his head:
Idlestop. Ditched in a fosse to the Trent.
The NCB cracked the aquifer. The NFU
have it cracked both ways: they drain
and pump as suits. Defoe's 'little but pleasant'
river, now littler and unpleasant.
The inland port of Bautry is no more.

The Scrooby Congregation, shredded on the grilles
of the Stockwith pump, dumped bankside
with the dredger's eels and Bob Roberts'
monster roach. Rædwald buried at Sutton Hoo,
the Northumbrian kings in Bede. The allures
of Rome, its splendour and consolations,
the promise of life eternal—they could take it
or leave it—Þunor's hammer knows best.

But Franks and Merovingians, alliances,
trade and riches—Augustine, Paulinus, Laurence ...

The Old Course fragment at Lindholme Lakes
is a hundred yards across. Stocked with hare-lipped,
specimen carp. Imagine the river in 1626,
from Markham to the Mere—broad tidal waters,
clouds of fowl, shoals of upstream salm—
nightfall on the reptile fen. Lindholme,
Moorland, Hatfield Lakes—locked down:
the stag-heads and werewolves are stalking.
Lower the tip of your split-cane rod:
these peatland drains are black with little eels.

Hæðfeld
633

Four-three up in the April duskfall,
away at Hatfield Borstal. Five minutes
on the referee's stopwatch. Crowd pressing
to the touchlines—*smash your fucking face in!*
William Whitelaw's short-sharp-shock:
black boots, white shirts, grey trousers—
short-back-and-keep-your-neck-clean. Everyone
back for a corner. Inswinger, front post, *up*—
sparked-out in the six-yard box. [Screws and trainers
racing on, smelling salts, commotion.]

Snigling eels in the snaky lake on the Lings
by Carr Side Farm. *Piscator:* scholar,
cleave to the dark of the alders, lest
the king of Gwynedd confiscate thy tackle.

Venator: I have nothing but string and a bent pin.
Two corpses float in Ophion's pool.
Edwin floats face up. Wilfrid floats face down.
Venator: the first turned against Wotan.
Piscator: the second against the eel.
[The ref's ACME Thunderer chaired
bold Penda groggy from the feeld.]

Winwædfeld

655

Midsummer dark-moon, black belly
of the Went. Clouds heavy with thunder,
a tremor of distant horses. Glyphosate
drifting down from the rape on a crisp bag.
Mackerel-baited eel trap, sunk under
the crampball ash; stake hammered
into the tangle-root, to hold against the flow.
Greasy, fish-stink fingers—Ulle's pestilent bootlace,
knotting to foam in my Vaseline fumbling,
nailed to the tree, lank and bleeding.

Waterhens shrieking. Mink slinking
in the sedge. Ghost-voles scuffle and plop.
Eagles over the viaduct, the screech
of tearing metal—the spiked head of Penda,
riding the roil in its gorgon diadem,
sinks in the silts like Eohippus, butchered
girth deep in the quicksands of Tethys
by baying Haplorrhini, hairs tearing
from dock-flesh and writhing to darkness,
through turbine blades, nets of plastic Sargassum.

Quo Warranto?

Úlfr: I came with the king and we took it. I earned it with blood. It is my right and my reward. *Spanner:* I asked him nice, then he had no choice. *Smith:* the woes of my people cried out to me. There is strength in combination. *Lumb:* I worked hard for it; if you want the same, do the same; stop whining for handouts. *Pharaoh:* the question makes no sense. I am the Universe, Alpha & Omega. *Norfolk:* the sovereign majesty of the people, the Pope and the Bastard. *Tupper:* bloomin Ada, where do I start? Varsity toffs, the Greystone Harriers, the state's monopoly of violence—*Brown:* fuck off! you're trespassing! *von Donop:* breeding, ludere causa vivendi. *Savile:* I'm a character, like Geoffrey or Peter—ur-ur-ur-urgh!—everyone loves a clown! *Thoroldsson:* shotguns and summonses, private schools and private property. */ˈstiːvn/:* the drained fen, the Wimpeys, the cellar. *The European eel:* I'll vanish or suck out your brains. Makes no difference to me.

eely

óðinn skipti hǫmum. lá þá búkrinn sem sofinn eða dauðr, en hann var þár fugl eða dýr, fiskr eða ormr, ok fór á einni svipstund á fjarlæg lǫnd

/ˈstiːvn/ could lie as if sleeping or dead and project his spirit into a hengikjǫptr, swimming in an instant across the maelstrom of the universe

snorri sturluson, *ynglinga saga*, 7

forwyrd

*bitten by an ichthyotoxic eel, /ˈstiːvn/ warps
into a weraal in the dark of each new moon. his
raiment is shadow, his habit is blood, his range the
rip of space-time. he roams and kills—rat-trap mandibles,
fishy stiletto, red bayonet in the cellar.
the weraal worries the gibbering civilisa
tions—evrything's slaughter, drugs or porn. he gnaws the fen
nish mandrake and stiffens like a clit—sting like a butch
t trinidad scorpion. the weraal is a brute
theosopher, an adept of his dna's sol
ipsistic wyrd. he has bitten his grimoire in the
vellum of our throats. thirteen times each lunar year his
snake awakes and finds itself the wet print of a man*

body of dark

[un]settles himself with breathing, bollwurz steeped in the
slime of eels. imagines anguilla as body of
dark: greasy lycra, rippled and flexing, dripping with
ditchblack crude. iris, disc of yellow flag, unblinking
silt-flecked patina; pupil slit to the shifting dim
ensions, agarthi and schamballah—adderfang, wolf-
maw, caligosaur. quick blur of star-white underbel
ly, the dissipating contrail of a comet, or
watcher—lilitu, slinker in shadow. fingers with
out hands, hands without arms, feet without ankles. fishtail,
fishy pudenda. inhabits the body of dark:
the weraal slips his scabbard—act of will, imagi
nation. lithe knife, swimming through spacetime's wild sargasso

behold the head of a traitor

over land and water, mire and kjarr, rasalhague, o
phiuchos. from the tattershall shirts of the cl
a to the archons of akasha. ranges wisely.
the unwary by dark and lonely water, dangling
from the boom of the yellow excavator, or flopped
face down in the lilypad duckmoat, stickleback fren
zy at the rippage in his throat—minky weraal kills
for the sake of killing; slithers from the duckmoat to
the privy of the king and drags him to the scaffold
through a mire of ermined turds, torn daughters of the tit
led and ambitious. headless basilisk spurting ne
matodes, detonating mine o' serpents—*stella nov
a.* aalwulf's protectorate, the soviet of fen

porzana

the night is young, the cosmos thirteen point eight billi
on years. the spotted crake drips in the blood-dark fen, tar
sus deep in powte fry. four fundamental forces, com
bining into nature cures for the sad and unex
terminated. the weraal knows nothing but photo
taxis and coppery haemoglobin. the spotted
crake's drip drip drip drip dripping purples the basilisk
into his pet-lip rage; he cannot command its un
tapped gold: enter cornelius, a man of many
parts—traverse, ascending and sigmoid colons, a third
of the basilisk's arable waste: snagged high and dry
in the turbry birches, gut-slash leaking threadworms—aal
mutter licks prehensile lips, broods in the coypu's hole

bloodspoor

the weraal finds the absolute night congenial.
in blindness he finds vision. he feels the vibrations,
homes in on the stinking pheromones. he cannot see
the spark of light. he cannot see the hypothetic
al soul. submarine anvils dully whumped, the small-boned
inner ear. capillaries pulse and flood the flesh with
blood. which is life and therefore hypothetical soul,
sealed within the breathing skin, in wracks of venous gri
stle. no blood—no life, no sustenance: the dead provide
neither nourishment nor release. craves lipids, fuming
oxygen, white phosphorous in suspension. fangs rise
and fall on heartbeat's leaping altar. cities of shift
ing greyscale, impossible planes and geometries

pull down thy vanity

the anxieties of the weraal in the days of
the visible moon. he is not the weraal: he is
/ˈstiːvn/. it pleases /ˈstiːvn/ to think he is an eel,
but he is not an eel. which begs a further question.
why does he allow the universe to kick sand in
his face? [that is not the question.] to deep hook him and
rip out his cringing intestines, saw off his head, toss
him into the flow? he thinks he is sad because that
which he loves is reft from him. he thinks he is sad be
cause that which he loves is kept from him. he thinks he is
sad because he is not mad. blades rust, ropes fray. the wer
aal broods in his cave by day and on evil inter
stellar nights. he lashes out, retracts his blade, and hides

the patience & faith of the saints

the weraal is packing his asymmetric rucksack:
opinel skinning knife, army surplus fairbairn-sykes,
spear & jackson ten-inch tenon; hultafors hatchet,
felco cutter—cable ties, assorted; disruptive
slub, size 5 air-bomb repeater. who is like unto
the weraal? who is able to make warre with him? the
weraal's eyes are onyx, his jaguar daggers huit
zilopochtli obsidian. south pump's black mirror,
a pane of liquid pitch. croak and squeak the music of
the night: woodcock, long-eared owl. the stuck pig screams of rails.
the weraal's scream is silent, his bracken-slinking mute.
heat sig cooled to ashes—he wasn't even there. eve
n the spot of the cop helicopter can't find him

the cross of a frog

[tabletalk, when the table is a freshly slain tor
y being butchered by the river.] *weraal:* what's wrong
with the head is civilisation. i mean, no-one
kills out of anger no more, that lightning flash of an
nihilating rage—and the cbi pockets the
surplus. *aalwulf:* it's true—we're too attached to life. i
kept a tank of tadpoles and they et one another.
i watched them tear each other apart, ten-or-a-doz
en locked onto one, tails like shitting whippets. last man
standing was a frog. *aalvater:* which you crucified
in a calculated act of blasphemy [laughter].
of course, talking to yourself, when peeling an apple
by the river, is itself a sign of depression

ex nihilo ad nihilum

the singularity of the aalmutter refutes
the universality of natural laws and
the cosmological principle. her kaleido
scopic fish-womb wriggles with eelmatter conjured from
mystical γῆς ἔντερα, where annelids, nem
atodes and ammokoits gather to suck her milky
follicles. baryogenetic birth pangs account
for anguilla, her animate fish-flesh and anti
matter shadow. what lurks in the coypu's hadalpel
agic will obliterate the helix and her works.
eel and eelpout, stirred into extinction's primordi
al soup, the cornucopian endometrium
of the panviviparous universal mutter

moira

weraal and aalmutter sitting up a tree, k-i
-s-s-i-n-g—/ˈstiːvn/ said, too tame for me. wer
aal and aalmutter went down to the dairy/weraal
took out his hairy canary/aalmutter said, what
a whopper/let's get down and do it proper. slip on
the greasy black shadow, fiesta, says new forms ex
cite her—/ˈstiːvn/ and fiesta wriggling in the /grɑːs/,
eel up her fanny, lamprey up his arse. balmy corn
rig nights, under the warhead's creamy tracer. ice grind
ing from the poles. hibernaculum in the coypu's
hole. aalmutter, ripple in the cmb: /ˈstiːvn/,
marching with cnd: fiesta, let weraal watch
her pee, from the lemonade boughs of the kissing tree

10^{-43}

in principio anguilla—aalmutter, roiling
in the void. aalmatter, aalmutter's dottir. aalva
der, aalmutter's son. weraal, aalmutter's dottir/son.
aalmutter bites her tail. allmatter a blip in the
cosmic microwave background. /ˈstiːvn/ says that the depths
of the stcz might as well be mac
s0647-jd. he dreams the wer
aal at the edge of time, hunting giraffes on the shif
ting ripple, the mathematical fancy's non-ev
ent horizon. death chose him from before his birth, ten
to the power of minus forty-three. he's plummet
ing like livyatan, forty-five hundred fathoms
deep in the puerto rican trench. and then the comet

i do in all honesty love this world

æl-bopp was spawned in the oort cloud's cosmic sargasso.
argon, deuterium, scales from ymir's skull—aalmut
ter. something fuzzy in her coma, nuzzling the out
gas from the vent: aalvater, fat with panspermian
milt—acrosome, nucleus, middle-piece, tail. ophi
on's apparition in the world-egg's soft corona,
a spurt of milky star. vater und mutter, shudder
ing over the earthrise redds, shedding billionfold
draconids. /ˈstiːvn/ turns his face to heaven and his
cheeks run milty tears. weraal prowls from his darkside hole
in telah's doctored coma. locks onto the scent of
applesauce and phenobarbital. /ˈstiːvn/ prone in
dead decades. fishy auðumbla licks him into shape

jubilee

harrying the farms between broddy and vissett: by
water, askham, cook, *et al.* the proud cast on middens,
our beacons went up: rejoicing in the photic thridd
ings. or, trapped in the barn by hadal peasants, gammon-
faced demagogue torches—send for the syndicate's shot
guns! the barn goes up, and a shadow breaks out, crashing
the planks in a blaze of hay, into the fusillade.
he was through them already, bellying between green
wellies and hobnails, commando leatherette. pitchforks
aloft for the valiant guns and farmers—three cheers
for the sturdy yeomen! [is the aalwulf dead or mere
ly in the dark?] [something had to burn.] enter colli
ers bearing boxes of bud and trays of minted lamb

ararita

the silver reaper scythes him under mats of yellow
flag. hangs in the gloom of the chrysalid duckmoat, re
combines his bollwurz dna. the stripped bones of o
siris, the stripping teeth of seth: jackal saliva
and aalmutter magick re-quicken his coffin of
flesh. incarnadine lotus, cutting his cremaster,
floating to the light, where the short-toed eagle orbits
the sun, eels dripping from her talons. the excava
tor's boom is lowering the bucket, trenching in the
mass grave of the fen. /ˈstiːvn/ rises from the deadpool.
his boots bounce off the peat. his rucksack rattles with rus
ty ordnance, scorched neurocranium dim with ignis
fatuus. blood conjurations conjure only blood

Eelysium

Eeliptical Fencentricities

Storegga

I

'Oumuamua, tumbling in the galactic flow
like the lopped head of anguilla, breaking
the bounds of the fixing star, the grasp
of the lunging planets, her loosed crag
crashing through gravity's fences and coursing
to wing-finned Pegasus, the oceans
of leaping Equuleus. Tetherless mustang,
wild interstellar tarpon, unlassoed, unbroken,
roaming the range from apogee to perigee—
until Gamma Equulei's switchback aphelion
slings her back to Centauri's dazzling Sargasso.

II

Earth orbiting like a longed Lipizzaner,
a goldfish in a pool, eccentric, oblique,
precessional: the Milankovitch ducks
line up off Humber, flee south from the ice-locked,
shrinking sea to the deltas of Ushant,
where elvers ascending under the floes
enter the stream of the broad Fleuve Manche,
press on to the subarctic rivers of Rhine.

Earth nailed to the Sun like a hoary vulture,
a birch leaf trapped in the meltwater whorl.
The basking perihelion widens the ascent
from the Río de Oro to the Norwegian Trench,

the swollen lodes of Europe. Eustatic
Atlantic shoves back the estuarine outfalls;
meanders flatten in floodplains to fen.

Earth circling like an index finger
daubing red ochre, a pack of wolves
or howling men, at bay round a phalanx
of roaring aurochsen. Pelicans panic,
cranes bugle and trumpet, beavers
slap their rubbery platypus tails—
thirty-foot sturgeon ramming their dams,
salmon taller than men leaping over.

III

Reed hut above the oxbow, holme
in the cranes' black kjarr. Red men, bone hooks
and barbed harpoons. Cowhide coracles,
dugout log canoes. Pigs prowl the edge
of the campfire's glow, whelps licking grease
from children's fingers—earth-shudder
sky-split thunder: eyes lifted to the North:
horizon blitzed with shock-launched wigeon,
detonating greylag. The shivering hills stampede
with tarpan, washed down on the galloping tide,
maelstrom forests of ripped-out alder, tumbling
herds of white-eyed, screaming bison.

Daybreak in the wreck of Dogger. Gulls drifting
over the slowly rising sea. Seals hauled-out
on sandbanks, bleached ribs of stranded whales.
Dunlin and knot, swarming the mudflats,
armies of silt-spearing godwit and whaup.

Butterbumps booming from brackish phragmites,
gorged on the bootlace bounty. Harriers
quartering over. Campfire wisp from the holme's relief
in the pearl of the roseate dawn; boat slides
from creek into tidal waters, trailing
its fuchsia ripple. Paddles out under chatter
of pinking terns, the flushed conflagrations
of billionfold gyring flamingos.

Elverkonge

Gleam from the bottom of the bog pool:
a hoard of torcs, disarticulated vertebrae.
Inlaid fibulae, helmets, shields. Tipped cartloads
of spelt, spilled wheels of Maremmana.
Ram fleece, plucked-out nanny goat opals.
The treasury of the King. The trinkets of the Queen.
The tears of the sisters of Phaëthon.
Wobble in the onyx of the bog pool. Long blink
of a golden eye. Kid opened on the cotton grass,
tartrazine gutfat bright as dark anguilla.

Morimarusa

Brigantes, Parisi, Iceni, Trinovantes:
or the reed-wraiths preceding, haunting
the roke in the smoke of crepuscular campfires,
prehistory's glaucous gloaming.
                         Yew-sewn longboats,
cutting the fret from Humber to Medway,
sunk to the gunnels with weight of wool,

cowhides, salt-cod, slaves. Prows slicing the fogbanks
from Elbe to Scheldt, crossing the Morimaru,
caulked plankbeds stacked with pots and amphorae,
olive oil, wine and papyrus—Frisii, Batavi,
Bructeri, Morini.   Nehalennia's pro forma
insurance: doves and cockerels, Belgian hares.
Lutetia's boatmen had entered the depths
and knew better, or worse: hornèd Cernunnos,
squatting in the fen like the Goat of Mendes;
Smertrios snake-bane, flailing his firebrand fasces;
Tarvos Trigaranos, the Bull with Three Cranes.
     Women singing in the swamp's dark forest,
an army of roaring men. Publius Quinctilius Varus,
dangled head down from Bructerian alder,
face sheeted in blood from his opened throat
gushing into Albruna's visionary cauldron—
the Ninth Hispana, floundering the mire
between Danum and Calcaria, butchered
like stags and stamped into the peat for the wolves
and white-tailed eagles.   Angles on the Saxon Shore,
across the German Sea, raising their huts
on éaland's íeglands, in middan Girwan fænnen.
Their children romp filthy and naked,
but sleep content among the flocks—butter
and cheese, pike and salmon, pork and beef,
wild geese—Freyr and Freyja, one-eyed Odin,
feasting holme-from-holme: fenwatter roars
with foam of henbane beer.
                              Cain falters
at the eel-mere, his broke-back tithe of grain:

groveller to the Loaflord, eater out of dirt;
wroth, and a countenance like a slapped arse.
The wolfish men had no respect, for his offering,
or his rule.

> 28 peers, 59 knights, 10 abbots, 7 bishops, lawyers, clergy, esquires, ladies, their servants, attendants & retainers. Neveel's family, their servants, attendants & retainers. Local yokels, sitting up straight with their knives and forks, resplendent in their napkins. 2500 covers, course after course after course after course, right through the holiday fortnight. 4000 pigeons, 4000 lobsters, 2000 chickens, 204 cranes, 104 peacocks, 12,000 quails, 400 swans, 400 herons, 113 oxen, 6 wild bulls, 304 pikes, 304 breams, 6 porpoises, 6 seals, 1000 hoggets, 304 calves, 2000 pigs, 1000 capons, 400 plovers, 2400 ruffs, 3000 mallards, 1000 teals, 204 kids, 204 bitterns, 200 pheasants, 5000 partridges, 400 woodcocks, 100 curlews, 1000 egrets, over 500 stags, bucks and roes. 4000 cold venison pies, 1500 hot venison pies, 4000 dishes of jelly, 4000 baked tarts, 2000 hot custards and 'proportionate quantities' of fancies and cakes. 300 tuns of ale, 100 tuns of wine.

The Enthronement Feast of Archbishop George Neveel

They were all there: Savile, Boycott,
her off *Countdown*, the beaters off the shoot,
the shooters off the beat, Sutcliffe, Davies,
Jenkyns. Everyone had a marvellous time,
apart from that Nigel Farage—he had the face on
all night—Ahuitzotl, King of the Aztecs
(whose name means 'water monster',
or 'water thorny', apparently), had outdone
Trump, putting a mezzanine on his pyramid
and sacrificing 80,400 prisoners
to heart-devouring Huitzilopochtli.
He never got jelly and custard though!

Ahuitzotl enthroned in the iridescent purple/
green-black feathers of the grackle:
great-tailed, released into the prickly pears
by the mighty Tlahtoāni himself, having burned
the huias of Titicaca in Xiuhtecuhtli's fires;
slender-billed vanished from the marshes.
Water *thorny*? The spike-backed crocs
of Lake Texcoco, says Euhemerus of Rhodes:
Cipactli in Nahuatl. But Teocalli's heavenly
ribcage ripper was no microcosmic caiman—
I bet you think I'm building to a gret big
fucking eel. Well, no—*Lontra longicaudis*,
the neotropical otter. AKA the aquatic ocelotl.
'6 wild bulls'? Feral Maremmana, aurochsen
of the Chace. The wolves come off the moor
at night and drag away their children sheep.
Meanwhile, at the feast they're tearing pigs
and munching pike like corn-cobs—or *maize*
as the coyotes call it. *Panem nostrum
quotidianum da nobis hodie, perdona
nuestras ofensas.* Who invited these dogs
with monkeys' hands? Centeotl casts out
Caliban, releases Tiddy Mun. Burbot nowt
but muddy cod, sturgeon Loch Ness Monster.

Girvij

lurks like a burbot   lunges like a pike
slinks like a bittern   skewers like a shrike
stabs like a heron   blusters like a coot
belches like a natterjack   whispers like a newt
dives like a dabchick   dabbles like a teal
sinks like a cormorant   burrows like an eel
scams like a lapwing   prances like a stoat
sucks like a nightjar   humps like a goat
builds like a beaver   wrecks like a bull
gores like a wild boar   harries like a gull
soothes like a tench   plops like a rat
strikes like an adder   pounces like a cat
snores like a badger   dreams like a bear
lopes like a lurcher   flees like a hare
hides like a woodcock   smiles like a fox
snarls like a terrier   bellows like an ox
honks like a crane   shrieks like a rail
burps like a gadwall   whistles like a quail
steals like a magpie   hoards like a jay
looms like a sturgeon   scuttles like a cray
stoops like a falcon   swerves like a goose
back like the bustard   gone like the moose
bleeds like the alder   the pelican, the rich
weeps like a rabbit   kills like a fitch

Eeldorado

Eelizardbirth

Naughty paike, the one that trips and goes,
caressing her dotterels, feeding them
from her fingers: milk pobs, hemp, chopped
liver. No longer a lady-in-waiting,
in glorious pup with the long-delayed Prince
of the King, a seven hundred and twenty
month gestation. Two hundred and fifty
wait on her, primping her petticoats,
praising her folly, necking and spatching
her docile birds—served roast and glazed
with honey, a dainty dish indeed. Then lewters
and mynstrels, legs akimbo, broken waters,
ails and whines: *O death rock me asleep.*

She came out red, all over like a garment
of scales, flickring her tongue and hissing
at her sister—*this day I have seized thy birthright,
but found our line and treasury skant.*
Big-dick basilisk, his bursting vaults required.
Philip? Charles? Atahualpa? Moctezuma?
Have metal/lack mettle. Already a Prince,
taking any such gilded cock-end as her King
would shrink her into a dynast's broodbitch,
lord her to consort, quean. She came out red,
garmented in blood, her snake-hipped sycophants
tonguing her arse and pissing her gleaming
in showers of twocked Florensian gold.

Madre de Deus doubled her treasury,
2000% return. The response, as always:
'more booty'. Drake mired on his pallet
off Portobelo, dead of the crimson squits:
'we must have gold'. Nothing ventured, nothing gained,
say the joint-stock pirates of the Spanish Main,
the dogs and beggars of the Dutch Republic:
Muscovy, Cathay, East Indies. Russell
at Zutphen, hawk's eye on the black tilth's
10% per annum—dykes and levees, sluices, sewers:
Governor of Flushing. Returns to Thorney's
untapped level with the kleptocrats and hydrophobes
of Zeeland—Pedersen, Jacobsen, Alert.

Walter up the Orinoco, Francis up shit creek.
Ermined poets, knocking up ermined ladies-
in-waiting, lopping heads and piling potlatch riches,
jostling for favour, monopolies, rank.
Lynk: you can't do enough for a good gaffer.
Scargill: you're only as good as your last shift.
(Thatcher is dining in Dave Hart's pyramid
and thus unavailable for comment.)
She-wyrm shedding her flaking plaster,
prolapsed, weeping, foul as braxie mutton.
All my possessions for a moment of time.
Basilisk brooding on the bullion of the City,
the exponential Drakons of the bourse.

Baseeliske

Shat out on reekie's dunghill, toad-egg
squat by a pugnax-rooster. Hatched
in the syphilitic outgas of the father—
a pockish man, I could have died of his breath,
or what he shot into me—the bufotoxic
tit-milk of the Queen. Chrismed
with the phlegm of the gleeting priest,
in the leaping spunk of satyrs.
                              Ruff lekking
the ings like baroque stags, lunging
and lurking, vaulting and spearing,
barrelling breast-to-breast. Torn capes of apricot,
sable and mink, herding and mounting
their flushed little bitches, dropping frogs
down the throne of the polder: *Mary had a baby,*
she called him Sunny Jim, she threw him
in the toilet to see if he could swim,
he swam to the bottom, he swam to the top,
then he got excited, so she grabbed him
by the—
          The pretty blond boys are scuttling
reeves on the marshes—breathless petticoats,
limp in the ermine's mouth. Basilisk cruising
the bogs and sewers, the endless search
for the diadem's golden turd. His sire
was smothered with a clap-netted ruff,
let of the necessary blood; his dam lost her head,
but it fell in his lap. Caliban raising
the devils of fen, the witches of North Berwick:
'O polecats of earth, martens of air,

fitches of fire and watter'—*stynking wesylls all.*
I could have died of their breath, their fangs
that sank into me: basilard, heather-eel, ditch-adder.

Corneelius

Monarchs will have their mottos: stick it on a scroll, underneath the shield—*Mottos Regum Ipsorum Erit.* The Scotch king had two: *In My Defens, God Me Defend; Dieu Et Mon Droit.* The Scots might have been illiterate, but at least it was English. Both amount to the Sutcliffe defence—God told me to do it. Corneelius had his motto too—*Niet Zonder Arbyt.* As long as the arbyt was done by somebody else—a view he held in common with the king, who was in dire straits, and Corneelius dug them: *Geld Voor Niets*—the chicks were free already. And thus, for righteously bunging Prince VI-dog-I, that he might piss it up the palace wall for another couple of months or so—a statue for Saint Corneelius. In Grantham, maybe, or better yet—somewhere in the Northern Shithouse: that'll stand in lieu. But statues had gone out of fashion since the Three Amigos tossed Winston's Column into the Bristol Channel. Where now will the Red Wall's Enochite plebs parade their Union Jacks? Cap'n Tom's crowdfunder wasn't found wanting: and thus, for the expropriation and expulsion of the fenfolk, plantation and profiteering, ecocide and extinction— I name this ship the Corneelius Vermuyden School, Canvey Island; Vermuyden Way, Fen Drayton; the Vermuyden Hotel, Goole; the Vermuyden Serviced Apartments, Epworth; the Vermuyden Tea Rooms, Thorne; the Anton Mussert Marching Band, Lunteren, or Ely. *Kijk Naar Die Yoyos*—South Cambridgeshire District Council.

When Henry Prince of Wales visited Yorkshire in 1609 he was entertained at Streethorpe on the side of the Chace towards Doncaster, the residence of Sir Robert Swift. After one day spent in plain stag hunt, the chief regarder of Thorne and R. Portington esquire, having promised to let the prince see such sport as he never saw in his life, the prince and his retinue went with them; and being come to Tudworth, where Mr. Portington lived, they all embarked themselves in almost 100 boats that were provided there ready, and having frightened some 500 deer out of the woods, grounds and closes adjoining (which had been driven there the night before) they all as they were commonly wont took to the water and this royal navy pursuing them into that lower part of the levels called Thorne Mere and there being up to their necks in water their horned heads raised seemed to represent a little wood, and there being compassed about with the little fleet, some ventured among them, and feeling such and such as were fattest, they immediately cut their throats and threw them up into the boats or else tying a strong rope to their heads drew them to land and killed them. Having thus taken several they returned in triumph with their boats to land and the prince dined with R. Portington esquire and was very merry and well pleased at his day's work.

Hatfeeld Chace

Flat sump boxed by seven rivers—Ouse
and Trent, Idle, Torne, Don, Aire and Went.
Winding and doodling over their warps,
slow broadening to Humber. Syzygy
shoves the fat lodes back, twin aegres
bulging the eel's wide roads and rising through
the gates of Don, boiling over the banks
and fanning the waters to mere: Thurn, Brad,
Count and Messic. From Fishlake to Amecotes,
Airmyn to Misson, 'fenny and morische' land:
alder carr, ingas, ombrotrophic mire,
boatyards and punt-roads, sheep and grazing,
fisheries, swanneries, fleets of geese,
skies black with wheeling plovers; the Grig
& Powte, the Fowler's Arms, the Fleece.

    The King's deer, his keepers of game,
beating the forest to Bradmere from Sandtoft
and Haxi. Henry Frederick—Prince
and Great Steward of Scotland, Lord of the Isles,
Duke of Rothesay, Baron of Renfrew,
Duke of Cornwall, Earl of Chester,
Prince of Wales—stropping his dagger
and pompadour sense of entitlement.
Poets sang him into life with a hundred
thousand tallage, and dirged him into death
with the same—salmonella enterica
serovar typhi: the great leveller.
    Cornelis of Tholen, a devouring
and a lawless man, seeking Eldorado,
found his Princely analogue in the arrogance
of the Crown: and thus underwritten,
loosed his Dutch against the commons:
Vernatti, van Valkenburg, Corselis, Cats.
They let the blood of the commonwealth,
subject the land to rape.

> Depositions against Joan Jurdie of Rossington, widow of Leonard Jurdie, of Rossington, were taken before Hugh Childers, Mayor, Sir John Feme, knt. Recorder, etc., on the 6th February, second James I, 1604-5, the 18th April, and the 16th and 18th October, third James I, 1605; and at the Borough Sessions she was indicted for having on the 10th April, sixth James I, 1608, feloniously practised witchcraft and sorcery upon Hester Dolphin, and on the 11th June, same year, upon Jane Dolphin, the daughter of Wm. Dolphin; also, the like upon George Murfin, son of Peter Murfin, on the 27th September following. These persons are severally alleged by the Grand Jury, upon their oaths, to have died from the effects of her wicked arts.

                              The Widow of Danum,
sharming from the yellow fen, grieving
for her familiar stags and bitterns.
She conjured the heir's proleptic ghost
to the funeral of his brother—clattering
through the Abbey nave, head wailing
from his armpit, exhorting the congregation:
gold from the east, silver from the west,
jewels from the four winds: riches
for the Unicorn and the Lion.
                                        Rainsborough
riding Humber to his plaque on the Primark wall.
Penda's lopped noggin, tumbling in Went,
meandering to its confluence with Aire.
Don joins along the way, loaded with nuts
of its own: Hengist, Aethelfrith, Edwin.
Eels grinning from the sockets, feeding
in the matter of their pink and fissured brains.

> I was fishing the Went the other day. It is a narrow river not over six yards over, but the crookedest and deepest that I ever saw in my life, therefore it is rightly called Went, which signifys deep in Welsh. Every turn of the river makes a great bogg on the other side, on which the water is thrown by the current and there is delicate fish therein; but such quantitys of eels that was never like seen. Sometimes there will break out, or fall out of the hollow bank sides, when people are a fishing, such vast knots of eels, almost as bigg as a horse, that they break all their netts in pieces.

The Great Leveel

Argus bright as the Dutchman's sash,
flushed from the choked umbelliferous lode
between Pode Hole and West Pinchbeck,
spiralling up from the shivering peat
to the vaults of Elloe's empyrean.
    Ommatid split-screen twenty-twenty,
catadioptric eye: from Lincoln to Cambridge,
Crowland to Lynn, a million-acre watterworld,
blue ropes of Nene, Witham, Great Ouse,
looping across the sedgy veldt, meandering
islands and bloating meres, moating
the ramparts of abbeys and cathedrals,
raised on the golden warp. Dark herds of cattle
clot the drove roads south; tottery fleece-carts
trundle east to the staithes and piers of Hansa;
spoonbills lift like bleached flamingos,
wild horses of Camargue.
                        Jehovah pounds his anvils;
fen's wet furnace rings. High front of midges,
hammering trawl of swifts. *Dispar* drops
from the molten blare, shatter-gaze seized
by the ant-line voortrek—Danum-Lindum-
Sleaford-Bourne—from the ruin of Santoft's
impied Cape to the fortified bawns of Thorney's
Orange Free State.
                    Bright Argus of Elloe,
fallen to a drawer in the British Museum,
tangerine flutter-flags scorched to burnt-edge
copper. Ermine underwing, stoat-stole stained
with ancient urine—the slash of Vermuyden,

Oliver Cromwell, stale of the Jacobite kings,
pissing into the dikes from the Great Walls
of Derry, foaming into the canalised Foyle,
and all coming out in the Wash.
    Royal William over Whittelsey—
Papilio machaon. Japanese lantern,
stained-glass lattice, soot and clotted cream;
moon-phase scallopings, owlish planets,
fretwork, wingèd lancets—slit
chrysalid born of tenchy Asclepius,
surgeon to the Greeks, who diagnosed
sociopathic Ajax from the panshine
in his eyes, sucked the pus from Philotectes,
and was hewn in the fen by Penthesilia,
the Amazon mother of Grendel.
                                The triremes
of Argos, beached on the Whittel Sea's
staked-out Troad, enclosures of the dead
and dispossessed. Russell collected
their sanitised corpses and brought them
to Heorot, where they were buried
in the stacks with Tyrconnell and Finucane,
tossed on the bonfires of the Orange Order's
Nationalist Curriculum.

Eelimentary Tractaet van Dijckagie

Tyranipocrit

Knútr ravaged the land like die Grote Mandränke,
biting off coasts, swallowing townships, scouring out
mass graves.
      At Thorney he turned the flood, as written
in Ælfric's Hexateuch, the Historia Anglorum.
Lord of the springtide's blind conjunction, the raging
German Sea, God breathed in his blood and steadied
his sword—collected his Danegeld, erected his gallows,
drafted his warrants and treaties.
      Sermo Lupi ad Anglos:
bow down to Jehovah, His Tudors & Stuarts, their pirates
and party planners. The Lord delights not in an eelish heart,
but a surfeit of French lampreys—anguillids bite,
petromyzons kiss and suck. Both prone to losing
their heads.
      Τύραννος: grasper, devourer—man of blood.
Ὑποκριτής: actor, pretender, dissembler—mask.
Jackals eating from the sewage of the lyon.
      Prerogative ανομία, rotten with blood, whitewashed
to sepulchrous, poppy day δίκη: Bagehot, Dimbleby,
Encomium Emmae, Andries Vierlingh's Tractaet
van Dijckagie, realpolitik's Pook Hill PPE.

Balby Carr Pastoreel

Terry and Jono, fishing the Division Drain,
between the Stardust Academy and the Amazon
Centre of Dreams. Flat Camargue of Gypsy horses,
boxed-off with the Balby Carr—hard-hat Cat-plant,
pegged-out peat. Traffic roar from Junction 3,
dim bittern beyond the White Rose Way.
Hogweed swelter, four-spot hawkers—*when on Poteric Carr
the Butter-bumps cry, the women of Bulby
say sommer is nigh.* Tez peels off his soiled Jack Pyke
and sucks on his skinner: *when you're dealing skunk
to the Woodfield PRU, you end up in Hatfield PDQ.*

    Sheerside ditch, steps spaded down to improvised,
puddled muck podges. Keep-nets, boxes, twelve-foot rods,
bronze on float and feeder. Fathom or so of water,
six or eight yard broad, a straight-mile cut
through chest-high rape to the Eldorado link road
and the tagged-up concrete culvert to the fen.

    Tench rising, nowt biting. Mozzies and midges,
sudden quick flickering ditch of martins.
Sky purpling overhead—*there'll be rain, else summat waur,
when the Butterbump booms on Poteric Carr.*
Squall curtains through. The sedge-fringed strip
of green meniscus pings. Jono shelters
under his tented tracky and cracks a can of Stripe:
*when you turn up pissed in induction week,
your chances of becoming an Associate are bleak.*

    Rain-blur clearing over the M18. Vast sheds
calved from south's cold edge shimmer the haze
of sun's wet cyanide skies. Butterbump whomps
the fresh-rinsed level.

                      Reel in, top up the feeders, cast—

twin plops at the edge of the iris bed. Tightened lines,
rods resting on their idlebacks. Scarlet float tips
tense and still. Tez blazes up a skinner.
Jono cracks a can of Stripe.
                            Fluorescent blue light
of an Emperor dragon, patrolling the lode
like the cop helicopter. Warblers going crackers
in the tall phragmites. Scarlet float tips tense
and still—odd tumbling roil at the top of the water,
ten or twelve yards downstream—*big tench,
or a moorhen rising?* The surface bursts
like a belch of methane, and wrestling on the roof
of the churning waters, a cormorant hoisting
an eel as thick as a twelve-foot rod's cork handle.
       Gripped in the prongs of the snakebird's bite,
the snakefish spasms with frantic voltage,
shorting and sparking to shock herself free,
lashing around his trigger-cocked head
and muscly flex of neck. He sprags his paddles
against the brawl and plants himself at anchor,
and jerking his head on the tensile bend, lifts
her like Nehushtan—only inflaming her pythoness
frenzy. She loops around his scaly throat
like the spring of a coil-over shock absorber,
throttling his pipes and bulging his sea-green,
saurian eyes to goggles the size of a silver eel's
downstream blinkers.
                            The cormorant flaps and thrashes
the water, striving to shake off the eely garrotte;
but already her squeeze is starting to slacken
as she suffocates in air—one-by-one along her notochord
the anaerobic myomeres burn their glycogen and give.
The noose-loosened snakebird gapes and relaxes,

then seizes his airy advantage, yanking her rope-end,
lashing, unravelling, until she hangs lank
from the snap of his jaws, bruised and weakly twitching.
He throws back his head and cracks her like a whip,
slapping her thong on the greasy water
until her length goes limp. The undead snakefish
spasms and quivers, provoking the snakebird
to give the coup-de-grace—he stabs the brain
through the fontanelle with the ice-pick barb
at the tip of his bone harpoon. She hangs
from his jaws like a wet rope. He ruffles his feathers,
shakes himself off like a dog.
                                  Warblers going crackers
in the high phragmites. Bittern whomps across the level.
Airbus 320, gearing down its turbofans,
loaded with labourers from Vilnius, or Riga,
preparing for splashdown at Donny/Dee-Dah airport.
Scarlet float tips twitch, unwatched. Cormorant
sailing low on the water, trailing an eel
as long as his plesiosaur body. Killing is the easy part:
now he has to take her down—putrefying herons,
goitred with dabchicks, bitterns shrivelled
on the gullet-stink of dinner-plate carp.
He throws back his head on his terrorbird neck
and opens his thylacine maw. Bouncing and gulping,
he jolts her down, inches at a time—head and gills,
pectoral fins, long body to the vent—till only
her snaketail lolls from his gape, a tongue of wet leather,
gleaming like a flounder on the fishmonger's tray.
Gorged and exhausted, he rests on the water,
crossing his back with his bat-wing feet
and fluffing his raven feathers. Crop bulging
like a bag of boilies, throat thick as an angler's wrist.

Then the final sequence of jerks and gulps—
her tail is gone, and his mandibles snap shut.
    Terry puts his hands together. Jono raises
a can of Stripe. The snakebird rolls on the drain's deep ooze
and basks in their approbation. Bittern whomps
across the level. Hazy yellow Cat-plant,
clearing off the rape. Sinks and disappears.

Privy Counceel

King on the throne with a copy of Titbits,
going hammer and tongs with a Mega Luv Doner.
Court fanned around him on the shithouse tile,
like spaff mags spread for a tosser. Magnificent
devouring, My Liege, if I dare to be so bold.
Hear, hear, absolutely, indeed. Might we
haply have the hexalted honour of licking up
the Royal Drips and Scraps—

> *Robin Asquith, winder cleaner, squeezing out his shammy,*
> *peekin from his ladder through the open shithouse winder:*
> *give yer arse a chance yor ighness!*

King straining like a sweaty beet, bulging
haemorrhoidal. Pot thunders and splats
like a herd of stags swept down on the Fishlake mudslide.
Another Princely Turd, Your Highness:
truly the Anointed Shite doth stink
like Samarkand roses, glittering with emerods,
rubies and gold. Might we humbly
roll up our humbelous sleeves and hum
belly therein rummage and snorkel—

*Robin Asquith, winder cleaner, shaking his head in disbelief,
shouting down to his mate at the foot of the ladder:
them pooftahs is pannin the khazi for sweetcorn!*

King folds up his Titbits. Wipes off his mush
with the back of his hand, stands up
from his keks and presents. Exalted Majesty,
if it indeed Thouself should please, grant us
the fragrant and zephyrous pleasure
of fettling the sceptred Sheriff's Badge,
with salivary amylase bidet squirtings,
Izal tongues and Petal Soft Quilted
corny mops of hare.

*Robin Asquith, winder cleaner, retching from the top
of his wobbly ladder at the Greek Street blue film
coprophiles attendant on his King: sick as a fackin dog.*

King lets off a ripper.
Thank you very much.

Sea-worm

The yellow eel's a gut, a digesting machine.
Jaws gape, teeth grip, taste buds
test the meat. Oesophagus takes it down:
antagonistic muscle action, cilia,
oozed mucosa. In the cauldron of stomach
the snatched are dismantled by acids;
then the alkali vat of the coiled intestine,
a rendering plant of boiling soda,
where mortified flesh transfigures
to chemical bounty. Enzymes quicken

in the churn—esterase, phosphatase,
amino peptidase—fuming through the microvilli
and thickening the blood. What cannot be used
is dumped as trash in the rectal ampulla
and jetsammed through the anus.

The silver eel's a submarine missile,
a glittring metallic migrating machine.
Skin-tight neoprene diving suit,
greased with euryhaline mucus.
Fuel-fat packed in zigzag myomeres,
long-fin, long-haul pectorals: *orecchio negro*.
Does not eat. Absorbs instead
all non-essential systems, including
the gastro-intestinal tract; self-destructs
in her breed-and-die DNA's engines—autolysis,
phagocytosis, the necrotising anus.

She travelled from the German Sea,
in search of the Azores Current, the mesopelagic
slip-road to the North Atlantic Gyre:
which she found in Cenozoic blackness
among the seamounts north of Flores;
and where her nineteen balled-up inches of snake
were hauled up in the nets of a scabbardfish trawler,
in the gas-distended, external stomach
of a six-inch Chiasmodon niger.

> *Black swallower, cestodes, travelling in the gut*
> *of the black-teethed swallower, with wiggy hairworms,*
> *flukes and hooks. Ermined enterobes, packing*
> *the lobbies of the lower intestine—feeding*
> *on the trickledown of sinecures and power.*
> *O white devil, Tyranipocrit, how impious thou art.*

Commissioners of Sewers

The final poem of this sequence describes how the Crown, aided and abetted by sundry Lords, courtiers and adventurers, used prerogative power and the state's monopoly of violence to drain and enclose the fenland commons, extort, expropriate & expel the commoners, and auction off the commonwealth to privy investors. The Commissioners of Sewers would conspire with landowners and adventurers to declare a given tract of fenland 'hurtfully surrounded', contrary to efficiency and the national good. The Commissioners would then lay a tax on the relevant parishes to cover the costs of the drainage, whether the parishioners wanted the land drained or not. They invariably did not, because their livelihoods were dependent on their commoners' rights to exploit the fenland's bounty, and in paying for its drainage they'd be funding their own ruin. After the commoners refused or failed to pay the tax, the Commissioners would then impose the works, which were undertaken by landowners and adventurers, often with the active support of the king. Drainage & enclosure would follow, with the commoners' rights being unilaterally withdrawn and the plots sold off to Dutch and Huguenot settlers, whose loyalty—to their landlords, the drainage and the Protestant Crown—might be assured. The commoners' protests were put down with the full force of the state: militia and vigilante groups were loosed on the Enemy Within; dissidents were murdered, assaulted, imprisoned; 'ringleaders' were brought before the Star Chamber and subjected to astronomical, unpayable fines—equivalent to millions in current exchange value—resulting in committal to the Fleet for non-payment of tax and fine; unless, of course, they signed affidavits renouncing their rights and consenting to the drainage, at which point, tax and fine would be waived and the fettered might be released—to labour on the settlers' farms, or to leave their lands forever. Thus the 'Drainage of the Fens', generally characterised as a glorious feat of 'British' engineering that transformed unproductive, uninhabited and pestilential waste into habitable, rich and fertile farmland, able to feed the growing population of a go-getting nation on the rise—that is, as the perfect form of nationalist, capitalist, 'we're-all-in-it-together' progress—was in fact a ruthless act of imperial violence, ethnic cleansing and colonial plantation not different in kind to similar English or British atrocities in the Americas, Australasia, Africa, Ireland and Scotland. See also *Enclosure Movement, the*. The Scotch King, Man of Blood and pleonexic grasper cHARLES sTEWART was the primary instigator of this aktion against his subjects, but the following stuffed their faces at the trough: Francis Russell: percentage man, fence-sitter, Earl of Bedford; Saint Corny Vermuyden: gambler, undertaker, Ponzi fraudster; Sir Miles Sandys: parvenu, ring-licker, addled Parliamentarian; Sir Thomas Lovell: lumper, scrumper, Pode Hole pumper; Sir Philibert Vernatti: a Dutchman, Gentleman of the King's Bedchamber; Sir Jacob Cats: double-Dutch, knighted by the King on account of coin, adventurer and man-of-letters, 'more renowned than read'; Sir Robert Heath: pro-forma used-car ducker-and-diver —Archer, Farage, Johnson; Sir Edward Heron: bent copper, delinquent, gangster; Sir Anthony Thomas: swindler, debtor, man of mean estate; Robert Killigrew: privy-this, I-dub-thee that, farmer of corners and guaranteed profit; and his son, Sir William: vast gainer, Member of Parliament, *poet*— dissociation of sensibility in the dried peats of the coffy house, the emergence of the Poetry Voice in the Restoration court— elocute murderers, slavers and scammers, up for the Forward Prize. The poem is over. There will be a test.

Eelkonoklastes

Filth as thou art

The life-or-death prerogative power
of Ivan Karamazov's Master of Game,
wolfhounds loosed at the slipped boy's scut,
hauled down in the snow and torn in the jaws
of his ululating mother;
                         gold-rush garimpeiros,
lopping the heads of the Haxi Yanomami,
something about a stolen hammock,
their cleansing from the commons;
                         shish kebab
paedos, pimping and raping unlooked-after
AirMax scrubbers—panga wielding paki
ninnies, watermelon smiles.
                         Brit White Chief
getting out of hand with his taxpayer-funded
Brit White Bird. Well, asked Ivan. What does he deserve?
Boris stopped spaffing and thought for a sec.
To be shot, he muttered. But already his mind
was somewhere else

                       hunt ball interns,
indigenous schoolies on cigs and free dinners,
wearing Joop and 9 carat Yanomami lip-plates,
the stringbulb flat above Booze n News, choc
klet starfish dripping with garlic mayo—
*we're having a gang bang, we're having
a ball*, Rita, Sue and PetSu too, Leeds Tiffs
with Sav and Jayne MacDonald: inner sense

doubtful—at *that* age, from *that* estate,
at *that* time in the morning, with the eel fishers
baiting their creels in the boatyard,
eights sweeping the river from Kulmhof
to the Wash, Spinnefix singing his little white house,
the black band of Florian Geyer. Shot
in the beams of the Rothermere staff car,
which he smashed as he fled, a hole in his head,
to the lays of Ness Ziona

                        defacing the flyleaf,
Brer Rabbit's a Rascal, 1974:
thank God I was born alive, not dead;
human, not an animal; a boy, not a girl;
English, not foreign; and Yorkshire, South Kirkby,
the Wimpeys—RULE OK!—scoring his hat-tricks,
wheelying his Chopper, 100% on the test,
this Prospero of Osgoldcross, Ariel of Frickley Park:
Kirkby rec Caliban, proud as Punch
in his catalogue Falmers, boss-eyed, club-footed,
man or fish, legged with fins for arms.
The meanest, poorest and commonest sort,
that serve for the profit of conjurors,
and bleed on Dagon's altars.
                             Beacons ring
the changes. Bog-bull thumps the level.
Lads rip the pegs on Whelpmore Fen.
Commoner's muck.

Grendeel

The last English wolves roamed the mire
between Thorne and Crowle. Grew sleek on sheep,
the king's red deer. Prowled from the full moon's
winding gear, the 44,000 kilowatt windfarm.
The odd turfcutter, fisherman, fowler—kid.
In the end they were raptured.
                              Hughes at large
on Toner's bog, beret & M14; Nairac's shadow
at Altnamachin, Nelson on the Falls:
regnum defende. In the end, they were captured.
   William Bunting, roaming the mire
between Thorne and Crowle, leading his beavers
via the Front d'Esquerres and the murk of MI6:
semper occultus. SIS to NNR
by way of SSSI—armalite & ballot box,
direct action, torts. In the end

                    he was a rapist
and a nonce.
              The desiccating shoggoth
of the State, oozing over Haxi from the Idle
to the Trent, shedding eggs or dragon's teeth
like a protoplasmic burbot: Frenchmen,
Dutchmen, scabs—clubbed down in their dykes
and drowned with poles, bone-fires of their vanities—
five hundred commoners on the march,
caring for neither God nor King, and if the King
were there, they'd kill him. Furies flitting
between the ranks, baring their bosoms
and tearing their hair, showering stones
and imprecations. The shoggoth's militia,

firing into the Bogside and dropping Bob Coggan,
sending them singing with lead in their tails.

   Grendel hauling slaughtered Danes
to the halls of black Bethdagon, where the witch-hag
littered her fishy whelp—bald wolf with fins
and bulging eyes, swaddled in the slime
of his own prehensile tail. Dam unstanched
in the leaking fen. Heretics pressed
into bleeding peat, under the wickerman's hurdle.

   On Pohnpei, Bethdagon, they're feeding
their people dogfood. She hangs
beneath the altar, blinks her golden eye.

The Black Mirror

William Torksey had a lot to lose; turbary,
fishery, decoy, sheep. He loved the cranes
and wintry wigeon, the warp of the whistling
inland sea.
         So when the Crown conspired
with Amsterdam to expropriate his rights,
he sought a second-sight wench to prognosticate
how he might defy the schemers.
                The Widow of Danum,
bold Bill and the Hatfield commons, trekking
the waste to the scryer's well on the Lings
at Brierholme Carr. Stags fleeing before them,
crashing through blinds of high phragmites.
Terns wittering overhead.

                        Sphagnum sink-sump,
cotton-grass quaking: bow down at the fen's
black mirror—jet meniscus flecked with dust
and midges. Something chewed or eaten:
the humming of bees, in the air, in the ears,
the dry cave of the larynx—needle-shriek
of swamp-gnats biting. The men stand back.
Low spoonbill honks and shears away.
   One-by-one from her bosom they enter
the pool and vanish—askr, tade, grig;
the men press forward. The charm they may not
now or ever repeat.
                        Dark pane breaking,
releasing ignis fatuus—the wraith of the Magus,
formed from the wyrd-hole's smoking water:
Why hast thou disquieted me, to bring me up?
The men shrank back; the scratching reeds fell silent;
William wept his sore distress.
                           The wraith waxed wrath,
and the waters trembled: *Wherefore pleads thou*
of an Israelite, and not unto the Philistine lords
unto whom thou has sold thy trust? Thus the fen
shall be dried and put to rape, and thy head
struck off and spiked in the halls of Dagon;
and all of our posterities will shrivel like the peat.
   William fell to his knees and implored him:
Is there no relief for the widow's son?
The vaporous Magus rippled in the wind:
Four hundred years will the Dutchman's drought
afflict our shrinking land—then it shalbe
as in the days of Noe; the heavens will roar,
the wild seas rise, and the aegre rage in Trent and Don,
breaching the banks and wrecking the sluices,

gouging the sewers and drains. Rivers restored
to their loops and braids will flatten across the level,
drowning the red-leg partridge barrens
to swan-land, grebe-mere, pike-rich fen.

 William bent in van Valkenburg's rape.
Joan on her knees on the Yorkshire stone, scrubbing
for de la Pryme. /ˈstiːvn/ stares at his dark reflection,
a skein of bugling cranes.

The Ruin of Heorot

Pulpit axed to matchwood, nave a byre
for distraint cattle, herded among
the broken pews, splatting and lowing.
Bull-calf nailed above the altar—a sermon
in the English tongue—Raw & Wildman,
Freeborn John.
    Through the smashed-in teeth
of the window frames, the Portadown ruin of Santoft:
eighty pulled-down planter houses, dismantled
windmills, dammed-up dykes: sluices and bridges
swept away on liberated streams.
      From his billet
in the gable of the Pastor's manse, Prospero
conjures demons: Fenrir, Grendel, the shade
of Ahuitzotl—Nemmersdorf, Königsberg,
Victory in Europe—Caliban hauling off
Samsung flatscreens, stringing his Brexit bunting:
this is our Common, and you shall come here
no more, unless you are stronger than we.

Suspiria Regeelia

Big fish eat the little fish, but consider this:
that the Big Fish vomits out the lesser,
which in turn spew out their puke prerogative fry.
Princely power as Ponzi scheme—cash flows up,
shit flows down—keystoned in the mystery
of the Führerprinzip blood. Loyalist absolutism,
to each man his degree of power, dominion
and estate—capacity to hammer at the baitball.
Diminishing scale of coronets, rainbow range
of motley: monochrome diminuendo
@sportsdirect.com: grey Donnay joggers,
baseball cap—Puma King?—my, cashly.

Multiplying diadems on the chopper-edge
of death: earth's crown, crown of thorns,
starrie crown of glorie—he's lost his head.
His litany of peacock prayers: deliver me
from indifferent men, the insolent, mad and vulgar,
Cyclopick monsters, who nothing will serve
to eat and drink but the flesh and bloud
of my breast-fed Subjects, their Pelican
in the wilderness: wing-clippèd, half-pluckèd—
still clackety-clacking his whet and wetted beak:
fari vagnari u pizzu. Arbitrary Government—
the lawless Law of another's Will,
to which We Ourself give no Consent
… some men's Hydropick insatiableness …

Horror of water, madness. Not merely
Naboth's Boatyard, but the whole inheritance
deemed as waste that the rampant Crown

might seize it. The Commonwealth drained
in the gape of a single man: none were his friends
but pike and zander. Hoicked from the gimes
by forking rustics and landed at Whitehall's
Rumper Room—John Cook, or John McMichael.
Lopped and filleted, put on ice, till Oblivion's black parousia.
Rainsborowe coming on the clouds of Heaven,
pissing in the Orangeman's dustbowl fen. Ruff justice.

Enuma Eelysh

Gods of Storm & Abyss

Aethyric gears grind into place and lock
Earth's torrid horoscope. Sun's abyssal
furnace thrums its blaze. The world begins to sweat.
    The cedars are fallen, the clear-fell smogged
with the fumes of the heifers of Shamash.
The many-coloured roller suffocates in air,
falls foul of Shuruppak's exhaust throats.
    Explosive cyclogenesis, millibars
plunging, perigean springtide clawing
at the coasts. Adad rides the frenzied sea-beast
over the wall onto Humber's flat field,
the prairies of the Wash, where Nergal
and fierce Ninurta rage, throwing down
the Dutchmen's dams and dykes, and releasing
the raving Annunaki, black wreckers of Irkalla:
who uncorked the founts of the hadalpelagic
and smashed the panes of heaven.
    Six thousand square kilometre eelsea,
Huntingdon to York. Flesh clotting the sluices,
dumped on the gleaming warp: fowle and cattle,
creeping things, them that tilled the soil—
sucked downstream on the ebb like mullet,
devoured in the Mori Maru. Sunken farmyards
forming reefs; cormorants nailed-up high-and-dry
on the islet spires of Croyland—mute swans
sail the electric rail from Stevenage to Danum.
    Fragrant Ishtar, Quean of Harts, rose
from her bed and wept for her drownded people, *Woe*—
but Tiamat swallowed her up.

The Burbots of Guthlac

The powte to Peny Wisbitch: *little sister of the fen,*
thou hast been meddling in the Goetia. Mage and virtuoso,
invoking the Ancient Water Nurses, observing and recording
the habit of *Lota lota*—to spawn on the flood amid segg
and reed; a mean winter temperature of four degrees,
to quicken the boreal embryo; ditch and mire as nurseries
for fry; and flood to wash the codlings back into the river.
 Guthlac hooked his pouts with mandrakes, put them on ice,
wired them to his will: Holastri, Nimorup, Nominon,
the forty-nine servitors of Beelzebub, crawling from the Thames
like a legion of mudskippers, giant mottled eels of Feegee,
to wreck for their lives in the hydragoge library at Mortlake.
 Penny's shade in the Ark, fast on the mount of Croyland.
Ravens feasting on Ely's flotsam, dove smashed from the sky
by a Greenland falcon. Black rainbow over the Mori Maru.
And the burbots of Guthlac reported: *brethren of the fen,*
the desart of the Dutchmen is ended, the deathly reign
of the undertakers, sunk and overthrown. Flood rules with Moon
and Tupny Jack, the sinuous sisters of Ívarr's inland sea.
 Vermuyden's altar of cedar and myrtle, every cleane
and living thinge; Elohim clotted like flies at the blood-feast.
The drowned and the saved are the hermit's offerings,
the slaughterhouse of fen. Blown cows float with legs
sticking up like tables. Burghers clinging to tumbled gables.
The burbots of Guthlac, biting out proofs from benthic
Huguenot Bibles: *O smite the land for the water's sake:*
the dreaming of the eelish heart is evil from its youth.

Pantaneel

Cormorant yawns from the pinacle of the temple
and ruffles his raven feathers. Flurries in the wind
like the robes of the filídh, or falcon-breasted Freyja.
But that world is past. Beneath him the spooling meanders
of Humber fume in the purple dawn. Blots of pale horses,
megalith hulks of grazing aurochsen, heads buried
in the sedge. Gulls track the Trent, gold in the sudden
bright monstrance of Sun. Pink pelicans, rose flamingos,
lift. Cormorant drops from the turret like Wieland
and plummets the scarp to the broad lode of Linsey.
Splashdown on the liquid pane, shatters a raft of goosanders.
Peers beneath the surface glaze—plunged with gudgeon-
chasing grebes and crayfish-snatching dabchicks.

Frog-kicks deep to the reef of tumbled pylons, torpedo sleek
in his sheath and bubbling contrail. Eels lash and scoot
in the benthic gloom, vanish from silt-shot exit plumes;
mandibles snap on the wake of a hook-notched tail.
Snakefish crams in a crevice of the wreckage;
snakebird spears to the shattering portal and treads
the rippling mirror. Snakefish peeks and tastes the waters,
molecules in suspension—salt on the shove from the German Sea;
hydrocarbons leaking from the buckled tanks of Fina;
the Amitsoq gneiss and capelin scent of a bow-wave wall
of Atlantic salmon, travelling south along the Trent to spawn
in Don, Ea and Went. The run stretches back to Ravenser Odd,
a cordon fat as a motorway tunnel and thirty miles in length.

The milk and blubberfat scent of pigfish, ripping into
the upstream protein column, snowing the flow
with flakes of flesh—shoals of perch and roach zoom in,

spikejawed lunging pike. Salmon breaching like Trident,
swerving into the Don at the scour of Island Farm,
racing for the temenos of their redds. Bears wade the shallows
at Adlingfleet, plunging and spearing—cubs clambering
the weathercock on All Saints' floating spire. The fish press on.
The scar-backed pigs turn back. Bears gorged on fat
and gelatinous roe, red fillet tossed away—gravel banks
wick with black-back gulls and corvids. Osprey perched
on a half-sunk Transit. Foxes sitting on bony haunches.
A white-tailed eagle heaves aloft, gripping a flayed cock salmon.

Labours the level from Adlingfleet, gains height
over submarine Eastoft's lakeland: tree-tops, phone poles,
pantiled roofs—excited storks on gable woodpiles,
throwing back their heads and clacking their horny carrots.
Flap-climbs blind in the blizzarding whine of midges
and mosquitos, the thick air bombed with hirundines,
missile-swarms of swifts. Below, Crowle's reed-mere,
its bamboo maze of stampede paths acrash with sprinting deer—
silver plash in the sunk track's black, a hundred yards behind:
a file of wolves, fast to the cotton-grass scuts of the stragglers.
They close from Crowle to the towers of the trunk-sunk
Tween Bridge wind farm; where an eaglet shrieks
from brushwood shites on the hub of a seized-up turbine.

Hind splits off with her yearling calf, breasts the neck-
deep mire. Teal tear off the waters. The yelping pack
swerves off and plunges in. Heads grinning the swim
to the warp-dumped rise at the loop of the reborn Brier.
Hind hauls out on the mudslide bank, shakes off
the foul black water; calf flounders in the quag
behind her, bleating like a kid; head-grins gaining,
gleaming canines; hind barking stankside, shock-volt

lunge and rearing; calf-scream, white-eyed
howling mire—wolves converge like filthy sharks,
jaw-trap clash and snarling. Stunned hind trots off
along the turf bank, slips into the tangled kjarr—stumps
like sharpened pencils round the clear-fell duck lagoon.

Slap-tail warnings rocket off the pintail. Otter looks up
from his half-scaled carp. Magpies rattle their alarums
from the alders overhead. Beavers plunge the khaki water,
scattering shoals of loafing perch and vanishing up
their sunken log-pile chutes—grigs peep from every snag
and crevice. Cryptic lynx like a hairy goblin, peering from
the cut-zone's fringing trees. Magpies drop and heckle;
yammering blackbirds, screeching jays; hind passes through
oblivious, behind the high-stepping, stripe-head cranes,
stalking the sun-warmed stickleback shallows, their red merle,
hen high, pin-wing chicks, dipping the swarming fry.
Lynx crouch-stretches, edges forward; bare-fanged fen-fitch
backs off from his carp. The cranes have vanished.

High-stepping the kjarr into Moorends' flashlands,
skewering frogs and voles. Top ridges of the solar farm
barely breaking water, the crossbars of the Welfare Ground,
a foot above the ripple. Beyond the gime at Warplands Farm,
Okavango sedgelands to the overtopping tidal flats of Ouse;
blurry ungulates stud the plain, a scatter of erratics.
Whoopers cruise the Dutch Barn's shadow, pen and cob,
a litter of half-grown cygnets, upending in the algal soup,
plucking out pondweed, diving beetles, the monstrous
Palaeozoic nymphs of Anax imperator. Pike rise like crocs
in the sunlit gloom, hanging their gaff-jaws, fixing the gaze
of their riflescope copaline eyes—rocketing up to the paddling light,
and launching through the panicking, thrash-wing surface—

Down feathers float and settle. Stunned whoopers cruise
the sucked-back mirror. Pike plunges gulping depths.
Flood-snared sturgeon, sucking out mussels and muck-plugged eels
from a lakebed dump of propane bottles. Winged shadow
on the water: head-bob, bubble-honk whoopers—sow looks up
from her rotovator carnage, humbugs scuttle and squeal—
cream-crown drifts east, scanning the Marshland callows:
elk browse the club-rush swamp chest-deep in a dive-bomb
blizzard of terns; grebes slip off their half-sunk mats
and point their upturned daggers. Ululating snipe and curlew
wobbleboard the blue. Cacophony of quail and occult crakes.
Cream-crown drops the Ousefleet creek, frights up a resting cormorant:
struggles aloft with a bill-clenched wrestling tangle-knot of eel.

Hauls high over Blacktoft's inland sea, looks down
on the muck-brown flats of Humber, the ruinous
archipelagos of the fleets—windmills, water towers,
silos, snags—whited and streaked with ammoniac rookeries,
the whirling clamour of spoonbills and egrets,
pelicans, storks and herons. Shelduck clot the river
to the east, flap-scattered on the surge by a pod of racing
pilot whales, chasing the eelfare fast from the German Sea.
Joining from Ouse, a bulker from before, finally rusted
from its mooring at Goole, careering seaward on the swollen flow,
grinding shoals and clipping warp-banks, spinning
prow to stern, taking on water until the swamped hulk strands
on tern-blitzed Whitton's clamorous yarwhelp sands.

Gains height to cross the river, the flap-lode ford
to his scrawny brood on the Baptist's watch-cliff tower.
Eel twisting in his mandibles—bite-tightened horny grip.
Below, the ebb-tide's seal-basked reef at the rubbleheap
Trent Falls training wall. A blur beyond on the span

of the twin-towered, kittiwake-crusted bridge—a million bison
travelling north to their calving grounds on the Wolds
between Wharram and Warter. He wheels, begins
the glide to landing—smash of iridescent feathers,
high above the confluence with Don—snakebird falling,
legs and wings akimbo. Snakefish flung free and tumbling
like a rope. Cormorant crashes on the foreshore. Eel splashes
in the Trent. Greenland falcon circles down. Apoplectic redshank.

Skull-slammed, nerve-shocked notochord—the dropped eel
shuts down, temporarily on the blink. Sinks to the submarine
delta of the Don, its fanned-out drift of washed-down tractors
and shoals of skeletal Dutch—the seventy-seven-fold
heirs of Lamech, their hybrids, growth and windfarms.
What are these worms that are their eyes, the intercostal lacings
of their ribs? Comes round in the sockets of a Huguenot farmer
or playground-raptured child, and coils in the cranium, lunging
in the darkness of the current—hoglice, caddisflies, loaches, bleak—
bulking up the biomass of eel. Bears dive and rummage
among the bones, tear out the saving flesh; fish follow
in the rinsing blood and wake. All mouths partake and are renewed.
Coiled in the cranium, lunging in the darkness of the current.

Dreams of Sturgeon

I

Running lead-legged along Chequer Road
with sturgeon pit-gripped under each arm like carpets.
Smash-and-grabbed from the Don diorama,
the dusty basement stacks: two stiff and dripping
formaldehyde fish, gill-gaping back to life.

Town Hall hue-and-cry—alarms and sirens,
racing footsteps, shouts going up like tracers:
curators, councillors, nightclub doormen,
bobbies with fiery torches, yells—*No unauthorised
reintroductions!* Echoing blurs of tangerine
streetlights, bruised cumulonimbus skies.

Septicaemic sunrise on the floodplain of the Went.
Chlorine fogbank, manhunt closing:
Those antique fishes belong to England's Queen!
Stumble-lurch across the tussock—weak knees
begin to give. Girthy sturgeon, armpit twisting—
wriggle-flex gaping fish. Scuff-trips, stagger reels,
quads and biceps failing—*We've got him now!*
Lunging Bridewell rakes the burglar's shoulder—
dives headlong forward, grip released:
sturgeons skid the warp-bank mudslide,
split the viscous liquorish of the Went.

Crocodile shark-back breaking water,
heterocercal caudal fin, row of bony scutes.
Sinks the shallows and skims the silt,
trailing its barbels under the upcurved nostrum.
Projectile jaws crush swans and snails
slurp out bootlace, bullhead, loach.
Feeds in the broadening, estuarine flow
to the shellfish shallows of the German Sea,
the bathymetric oyster beds of Biscay
and the continental shelf.

II

Big broodfish winter at sea: enter the river
each spring to seek their redds—Gironde, Garonne,
Dordogne. Everything's against them: bycatch,
gravel works, Golfech's hydroelectric plant
and pressurised water-cooled reactors.
No wild breeding since 1994. A few dozen ageing fish,
anxious under the high dam wall, posterity
rotting inside them. Dissipate back to sea
in summer. Each spring fewer and fewer return.

Born in the Garden, died in the Flames,
Cain's spree-kill, carbon-offset Endtime.
Ninety million years of life, two hundred years of death,
coming down every year to a single fear:
will this be the spring that none return?
Harvesting gametes and raising fry in sterilised
plastic laboratory tanks, restocking the rivers
with smolts and two-foot tagfish: Garonne
and Dordogne, Oder, Elbe, Rhine—Ouse?
Nene? Trent? *Merely a vagrant in English waters.*
No unauthorised reintroductions.

III

I was flying about, over the Went, looking down
on its emerald torrent: squadrons of sturgeon
were piling upstream, armoured torpedos
demolishing dams, exploding weirs and sluices.
Stag-heads stalked the hardcore shoals, spearing
out the plenty. Gull-blitz swarmed the rips and scraps,

rose to meet my lowering. A black-back lunged
from the yelping roil and tore away my abdominal wall,
unravelling coils of nacreous intestine.
I tumbled down the greasy ropes into waters
slick with milt and caviar. Disrupted
in the stony shallows, a fillet of fallen man.
Hoovered in the suction jaws of dead Cretaceous fish.

Πάντα Ρεελ

Miraculous draught of yellow eels,
hauled up from the brick weir's plunge pool.
eBay crab-creel flexing and straining,
sheer weight of bulging mesh. Zipped-out
bankside, the knot unravels, gushes across the grass:
narrowheads, broadheads, grigs and gluts,
a three-foot, wrist-thick monster. Bootlace
dribble back into the stream like maggots.
The big eels slide through the nettle beds,
plop into the beck like a volley of diving voles.

Launch into the Pump, once more let down
your creel: a great multitude of fat anguillids:
the net brake, and the eels returned to darkness.
If he aske a fish, will hee giue him a snake?
Who raised these chain-link fences along the canalised,
sheer-walled beck? Who nailed up the KEEP OUT signs,
tore out the streamside trees? Who sunk the Pump
and raised the thousand-acre massif of ripped-out
Permian spoil? Topsoiled, landscaped, planted:
the thousand-acre Frickley Country Park.

Look down from the summit of Common End tip,
on the confluence of Frickley beck with Ea:
warp-rich floodlands studded with puvved-out ponies.
Beyond, the great yellow earth-machines
are tearing at the green belt, preparing the ground
for the thousand-acre warehouses of NEXT.
Six thousand jobs, six thousand buried in spoil
beneath your feet—cloudless autumn empyrean,
great silver disc of midday moon presiding.
Jet-plane contrails streak like exhaust comets.

Ea speeds to Don through Dutchman's cash-crop
windfarm. Eels mass her banks like skinny horses,
ready to break on the Miocene surge for Sargasso:
Harvest Moon, low water, holds them back.
Sky darkens bright with ancient light from uncountable
pinprick galaxies, where 'Oumuamua is lost in space,
swept blind in the Big Bang's current. A little eel
slips off, begins to make her way downstream.
Pike and cormorant, SpaceX Corp, are anguilla's constellations.
Stars explode and lurch for Earth like serpents.

Notes and Glossary

Eely is a symphony in four movements. The first movement, *Eel*, focuses on the lifecycle, ecology, epic migration, conservation status and enigma of the European eel. The second movement, /'i:laɪ/, explores two main themes: the author's autobiographical encounter with the eel, and the conflict that was so often associated with that encounter. The third movement, *eely*, develops the themes of the second movement in a guerrilla-pastoral, folk-horror fantasy of the author as a were-eel—if *Eel* is an adagio and /'i:laɪ/ a sonata, then *eely* is a capriccio. The fourth movement, *Eelysium*, concludes the piece and broadens the vision with a focus on the Eastern fenlands of England. Fenland—the mosaic of habitat types associated with lowland river systems in their natural state, including meandering and braided rivers, meres and lakes, marshes, bogs, swamps, reedbeds, meadows, mires, wooded islands, alder carr and birch scrub, all subject in varying degrees to annual inundation—comprises the richest and most ecologically diverse landscape in nature, and formerly characterised the lower catchments of all eastern English river systems. The English fenlands were once a stronghold of the European eel, as they were for many other species. The poem imagines the origin of the fens in the eustasy of the early Holocene, their development from the Mesolithic to the Early Modern period, their ecological and economic superabundance, the social and ecological catastrophe of their destruction, and a vision of their restoration.

Eel

The European eel (*Anguilla anguilla*) is a critically endangered fish that until the 1980s comprised up to 50% of the piscine biomass in some European river systems. In England, eels were staples of the national diet until well into the 20th century and were so valuable that many estates and individuals paid their rents and taxes in eels. Over the last fifty years, European eels have experienced a catastrophic decline, with recruitment of young eels to some catchments reduced by 99%. In 2013, the European eel was assessed as Critically Endangered by the International Union for Conservation of Nature and Natural Resources (IUCN) and placed on its Red List. The reasons for the European eel's decline include a range of anthropogenic factors, including the impact of the absorption of chemicals, drug metabolites and heavy metals on the fish's physiology and reproductive capacity, commercial over-exploitation, debilitation by introduced parasites and the impact of global warming on ocean currents and spawning conditions. However, it is probable that the main cause of the decline of eels is the destruction, degradation and debilitation of their freshwater habitat: drainage of ponds, marsh and fen; fragmentation of river catchments by weirs, dams, sluices and hydro-electric plants; water abstraction from rivers for urban, industrial and agricultural purposes; pollution from agriculture, industry and sewage works, and the intensive management of watercourses—dredging, straightening, embanking and culverting.

PAGE ELEVEN. The **Subtropical Convergence Zone** (STCZ) of the **southern Sargasso**—a vast area, comprising hundreds of thousands of cubic miles of ocean—is the spawning ground of the European eel. The Sargasso Sea is a discrete body of water located roughly in the middle of the northern Atlantic Ocean. It is the only sea that is entirely bordered by water—the current system of the North Atlantic Gyre, which circles around it, fraying its edges, but effectively corralling its warm, highly saline waters, and preventing them from significantly mixing with the generalised Atlantic water mass. The STCZ has three main characteristics that make it attractive to eels: the water is warm, allowing rapid embryonic and larval development; ocean currents bring nutrients which enable the proliferation of the zooplankters on which the larval eels feed; and the currents can be relied upon to transport the larval and juvenile eels to the European estuaries and rivers in which they will spend most of their adult lives.

Until the 20th century, the life cycle of the European eel was a mystery. In natural conditions, anguillid eels only become sexually mature in the depths of the ocean (to this day, no-one has ever encountered a sexually mature European eel outside of artificially matured specimens in laboratory aquariums). This led to the development of a range of theories about the origins of eels, from Aristotle's assertion that they emerged from γῆς ἔντερα (often translated as 'the bowels of the earth', although a more dynamic translation would be 'pond mud'), to speculations that they developed from horsehair, or freshwater worms, or that they gave birth to live young at multiple, unknown, offshore locations. In 1922, the work of the great Danish biologist Johannes Schmidt (building on the previous work of Francesco Redi, Carlo Mondini, Johann Kaup, Salvatore Calandruccio and Giovanni Grassi—the latter two of whom, in the late 19th century, demonstrated that a marine organism hitherto known as *Leptocephalus brevirostris* was actually the larval form of the eel) culminated in his identification of the Sargasso Sea as the spawning ground of the European eel. Schmidt did not observe spawning eels in the Sargasso. He came to his conclusion by systematically measuring eel larvae in the northern Atlantic and concluding that the area where he found the smallest (the most recently hatched) was the most likely spawning area. Subsequent research has refined and confirmed Schmidt's findings, and although spawning is still yet to be observed, it is virtually certain that the European eel breeds in the STCZ, north of the Windward Islands, 50-70 degrees west and 20-30 degrees north. In 2022 an international team led by Ros Wright of the UK Environment Agency demonstrated for the first time what has long been hypothesised, when radio-tracked eels trapped and released in Azorean rivers swam towards and entered the Sargasso.

Marine **snow** is the name given to the continuous shower of organic detritus that falls from the upper layers of the oceanic water column. Eels probably spawn at around **fifteen hundred feet**. Oceanographers divide the ocean into five broad layers, related to depth and the degree to which sunlight can penetrate. The photic layer, from the surface to around 200m, is known as the **epipelagic**. Below the epipelagic is the *mesopelagic*, which extends to 1000 metres. Although some light penetrates the upper reaches of the mesopelagic, it is essentially dark. Leptocephali travel in the upper mesopelagic and the lower epipelagic. Adult European eels migrate in the mesopelagic and probably spawn in its upper reaches. The other ocean layers are the *bathypelagic*, the *abyssopelagic* and the *hadalpelagic*. **Photocline**—the 'light boundary' between the epipelagic and the mesopelagic.

PAGE TWELVE. **Eighteen-degree water** is a body of water in the Sargasso that maintains the temperature implied by the name even when surrounding waters are much colder. The life-cycle of the European eel has eight, or possibly nine phases: 1. birth in the Sargasso and existence as a **leptocephalus**; 2. migration into continental waters as a leptocephalus; 3. metamorphosis of the leptocephali into minute transparent eels (glass eels), which soon gain pigment, and are then referred to as elvers; 4. invasion (or *ascent*) of elvers into estuaries and freshwater systems; 5. metamorphosis of elvers into yellow eels; 6. growth of yellow eels in estuaries and freshwater systems; 7. metamorphosis of yellow eels into silver eels, and the beginnings of the development of male or female sexual maturity; 8. migration (or *descent*) of silver eels from freshwater to the Sargasso, during which period a further metamorphosis into nuptial livery/physiology (phase nine, or perhaps the completion of phase eight) takes place after arrival in the ocean, but prior to mating, after which latter they die. The evolution from leptocephalus to silver eel typically takes place over a period of about ten to twenty-five years—the typical male begins silvering after about eight years in freshwater, whereas females begin the process after about fifteen years. However, many eels live as yellow eels for much longer than this—some kept in captivity have lived to the age of seventy or more. **Bright lens of brine … Antarctic Bottoms … North Atlantic Gyre**—the warm saline waters of the Sargasso are three feet higher in the centre of the Sea than at the edges, due to the action of the North Atlantic Gyre. The Sargasso sits on a layer of freezing water that originates in currents exiting the Weddell Sea. The five **Grumman Avengers** of Flight 19 disappeared in the Sargasso's 'Bermuda Triangle' on 5th December, 1945.

PAGE THIRTEEN. The **Deep Scattering** Layer (DSL) of the ocean is a phenomenon caused by the mass migration of oceanic creatures from the mesopelagic to the epipelagic in the hours of darkness (to feed) and a corresponding return migration to the mesopelagic in daylight (to avoid predators). The mass of creatures involved in this 'diel vertical migration'—plankton, small fishes, shrimp, squid, etc—is so great, it shows as an entity on radar. Leptocephali rise and fall in the DSL with the other creatures. **Phototaxic**—eels have five taxes, or reflexes, which manifest in different ways at different stages of their life-cycle: *halotaxis* is reaction to water salinity—ascending eels are attracted to less saline water, descending eels to more saline water; *phototaxis* is reaction to light—eels always seek to avoid light and cleave to the darkness; *rheotaxis* is reaction to currents—broadly, ascending eels swim against the current, whilst descending they swim with it; *stereotaxis* is reaction to contact with solid bodies—eels prefer to live and travel along banks and bottoms; *thermotaxis* is reaction to heat—eels are much more active in warm water than in cold, a clue to their origin as a tropical species. It is thought that one of the ways European eels identify their breeding grounds is by the elevated water temperature. **Deepwater Horizon** was the BP oil-drilling rig that blew out in the Gulf of Mexico in 2010, causing one of the biggest marine pollution events of modern times. The **Gulf Stream** is an ocean current running north along the coast of North America. At its point of maximum flow, off the Carolinas, its volume is around seventy million cubic metres per second—3,500 times greater than the flow of the Mississippi. Its velocity diminishes as it turns eastward at Cape Hatteras. Off Newfoundland it loses much of its thrust and diffuses into general North Atlantic Drift. **Oestrogen … neonicotinoid run-off** refers to the potential of hormones and chemicals to interfere with eel physiology and reproductive biology. 90% of eels are hermaphrodite on hatching (the remaining 10% are born definitively female) and only take on definitive sex during their freshwater phase. It is thought that exposure to anthropogenic oestrogen via sewage outflows may result in disproportionate numbers of hermaphrodite eels becoming female, with obvious implications for breeding success.

PAGE FOURTEEN. **Panamax freighters** are the largest cargo vessels able to pass through the Panama Canal. **Atlantic's Niño** alludes to the Pacific-based current and climate phenomenon, El Niño, and refers to the possible disruption to the Gulf Stream that may occur if the planet continues to warm. **Grand Banks**—the formerly rich fishing grounds off Newfoundland, which saw the collapse of **cod** stocks to 1% of historic levels in 1992, and which, in the late 18th century, saw the virtual extermination of the **Greenland right whale** and the total extermination of the **Great auk**, whose last stronghold was **Funk Island**. Before the arrival of European colonists, Newfoundland's native **Beothuk** Indians would paddle thirty hazardous miles to Funk, where they would take sustainable harvests of the island's millions of nesting seabirds, including Great auks, as part of their subsistence economy. The colonists, however, camped out on the island for months and took huge quantities of birds for commercial purposes—meat, oil, eggs and feathers—they even improvised rendering plants on the island. The flightless Great auks were particularly defenceless against this onslaught, and by 1780 were extirpated from the island. After the destruction of the relict Icelandic population in 1844 (by collectors), the Great auk became extinct, fifteen years after the same fate befell the Beothuk themselves—Shawnadithit, the last Beothuk, died of tuberculosis at St. John's, North Labrador, on the 6th June, 1829. She and her people were harried out of their lands, murdered and enslaved by settlers, as well as being killed in huge numbers by the European diseases against which they had no natural immunity. The **Gaels of Uist** were forcibly deported from their homeland in the 19th century by their absentee landlord, John Gordon of Cluny. They were transported to Nova Scotia, where they were abandoned.

PAGE FIFTEEN. The **North Atlantic Drift** is the North Atlantic's dominant north-west current. Unlike the Gulf Stream, which is wind-driven, the North Atlantic Drift is **thermohaline**—that is, the direction and speed of flow is determined by surface water temperature and salt content relative to other water masses. **Western Sahara**—the North Atlantic Drift carries some European eels to North Africa, although the vast majority arrive in European estuaries and rivers. Some European eels also find their way into Asiatic river systems via the Mediterranean and Black Seas. A **cetorhine** is a Basking shark. It has long been asserted that leptocephali are **helpless drifters** on the currents, unable to swim directionally. However, recent research has confirmed that which many have long suspected, that they are capable of directional swimming to a limited extent. The metamorphosis to **glass eel** that precedes the invasion of continental waters—**they somehow drop invisible anchors and hold / against the flow**—has been understood as implying a kind of deliberate halt. Exactly how and where it happens is yet another of the mysteries pertaining to the life cycle of *Anguilla anguilla*. **Myomeres** are the chevron-shaped blocks of muscle in leptocephali (and in most teleost fish) that develop into the spinal columns of elvers and eels.

PAGE SEVENTEEN. The **Weichselian** is the name given to the last European ice age, which definitively ended around 11,700 BP. **Gadoids** are fish of the cod family. **Ívarr** the Boneless was the Viking king who led the Great Heathen Army that conquered and settled much of England. He and his army entered the country in 865 via the Humber.

PAGE EIGHTEEN. European eels are *euryhaline* fish, meaning that that they can tolerate a wide range of salinities and thus pass easily between salt and fresh water. They are able to do so primarily because of the **mucus** they are coated in, which mitigates osmotic pressures and helps them maintain internal isotonicity. The **toxic** blood of the European eel contains a poison named ichthyotoxine, which is harmful and potentially fatal to humans if introduced into the bloodstream in sufficient quantities, through an open wound, for example. It is thought that ichthyotoxine's anti-pathogenic qualities help eels to survive in the bacteria-laden waters in which they often live—the *toxic* function of the blood has a *tonic* function in relation to the health of the eel. **Three Ridings and Five Boroughs**—the Viking divisions of Yorkshire and the Mercian Danelaw, that is: the North, West, and East Ridings of Yorkshire & Lindsey, and the Boroughs of Derby, Leicester, Lincoln, Nottingham and Stamford. These areas are drained by the eely catchments of the rivers Trent and Ouse, which join to create the Humber estuary. **Eiríkr** Blóðøx was king of Norway & Northumbria in the mid-10th century.

PAGE NINETEEN. **Hand nets**, or 'dip nets', are essentially huge versions of children's long-handled fishing nets. They are the traditional tools used to harvest elvers. **Northfield's ... and Moors**—in the 1970s, the three 'houses' at Northfield Middle School, South Kirkby, located in the Yorkshire's industrial lowlands, were named for the county's agricultural Highlands. The **Dutchman** Cornelius **Vermuyden** (1595-1677) was employed by Charles I to drain the Yorkshire Fen in the 1620s & 30s. He drained Thorne Mere, canalised the three meandering branches of the Don into the single embanked drain of the so-called 'Dutch River' and straightened and embanked several other rivers and streams—in the process turning hundreds of square miles of fen into arable farmland and precipitating a social, cultural and environmental catastrophe the scale of which we might begin to appreciate if we imagine a similar atrocity being inflicted on Botswana's Okavango delta or the Brazilian Pantanal. He did the same thing to the Cambridgeshire fen at the behest of the Duke of Bedford. The **Amazon Fulfilment Centre** is located between the river Torne and the Yorkshire Wildlife Trust's Potteric Carr reserve near Doncaster. **Bootlace** is the name given by anglers to small yellow eels.

PAGE TWENTY. **Oligocene Tethys**—the ancestors of anguillid eels evolved in the Eocene and Oligocene epochs, between 30 and 50 million years ago. **Tethys** was a prehistoric ocean. **Thorpe Marsh** power station was built in 1959, on the banks of the river Don at Barnby Dun, near its confluence with the **Ea** beck. It was closed in 1994, but the cooling towers were not demolished until 2012. Ea is Old English for 'river'. An **anadromous** fish is born and spends its juvenile phase in the river and migrates to sea as an adult, thereafter only returning to the river to breed. A **redd** is the name given to a fish's spawning scrape in the gravelly river bottom, or to the spawning area itself. **Mindless, reliable, pot-luck currents … Tagus, Severn and Loire**—eels do not 'return' to the rivers their parents inhabited, as is sometimes asserted. They are distributed to the freshwaters in which they spend their adult lives purely by chance. An elver that is the offspring of, say, a male that spent his yellow eel life in an Icelandic river and a female who spent hers in an Italian lagoon, might be distributed by the currents to an estuary in any landmass of the eastern North Atlantic from the Tropic of Cancer to the Arctic Circle.

PAGE TWENTY-ONE. The European eel had evolved, or a species very like it had, by the **Miocene** epoch, around five million years ago.

PAGE TWENTY-TWO. **Dredged and piled … suffocating eels**—in the summer of 2011 a 400-yard stretch of the river Went was dredged and deepened near Wentbridge, West Yorkshire. I found over 250 dead and dying yellow eels in the heaps of silts that were dumped bankside by the excavator. **Richard** is Richard Rolle (1300-1349), the 'Hermit of Hampole'. **Robin Hood's Well** was a famous roadside spring and festival ground located on the Great North Road in Barnsdale, a few hundred yards above the Ea beck, near Hampole. Henry VIII held a tournament and games at the Well in the summer of 1541, on the occasion of the post-Pilgrimage of Grace submission of the Northern nobles. This 'progress' was the only time in his life that Henry ever visited 'the North'. He made it to Pontefract and Sandal castles before he got a nosebleed and turned back, but not before his fifth wife, seventeen-year-old Catherine Howard, left behind at Pontefract while Henry visited Sandal, took the opportunity to cuckold him with Thomas Culpeper, a moment of stolen pleasure which cost both adulterers their lives.

PAGE TWENTY-THREE. **Another crawling culvert**—the number of culverts (beneath roads, under railways and built-up areas) migratory eels must negotiate on their journeys is enormous. Because many culverts have 'lips' or shallow water at entry and exit, especially during periods of low flow, eels are often delayed or obstructed as they attempt to progress, and thus become vulnerable to predation—by otters, mink, cormorants and herons—even by smaller mustelids, waterhens, ducks, corvids and raptors. Eels are similarly vulnerable at weirs, sluices and at certain types of fish pass.

PAGE TWENTY-FOUR. **Tangle of tiny dikes and streams**—during my research for this book I trapped eels in watercourses that were no more than three feet wide and two feet deep, right at the extremities of the Went and Ea catchments. **The H&B spur** is a short offshoot of the Hull & Barnsley railway, closed since the 1960s. Its embankment curves across South Elmsall common to the site of Frickley Colliery.

PAGE TWENTY-FIVE. During the 1980s and 1990s, the Victorian stone bridges that crossed farmland streams in South/West Yorkshire, and which often held bat roosts and the nests of swallows under their arches, were left to collapse, or were replaced with **concrete pipes**. The stones of the bridges the pipes replaced were typically abandoned in the watercourses.

PAGE TWENTY-SIX. The **Landrace** is a breed of domestic pig commonly farmed in intensive units.

PAGE TWENTY-SEVEN. **Inexhaustible biomass**—although European eels are still found in many rivers, in what seems on the surface like reasonable numbers, the calamitous speed of the collapse of their population is analogous to that of the Passenger pigeon, which once accounted for between 25 and 40 percent of the avian biomass of the United States, and which, as late as the 1830s, existed in flocks numbering in the billions. The population began to sharply decline (due to uncontrolled hunting, commercial exploitation on their breeding grounds and deforestation) from the mid-19th century. The last mass breeding took place in 1878, at Petoskey, Michigan, where as many as 50,000 birds were slaughtered daily for a period of several months. From that point the population of the Passenger pigeon collapsed, and by 1900 it was extinct in the wild. **Mijbil** was Gavin Maxwell's pet otter. **Toki** was a cheetah rescued and filmed by Simon King. **Christian the Hugging Lion** was purchased from Harrods by John Rendall and Anthony Bourke. He was later released in Africa by George Adamson of 'Born Free' fame.

PAGE TWENTY-EIGHT. **Nineteen inches … so conceivably a he, even from the catchment's far extremity**—female eels are larger than males (any silver eel over 50cm (19.69 inches) is almost certainly female and any silver eel under 40cm is almost certainly male, with mature eels in the 40cm-50cm range potentially either male or female). Female eels tend to penetrate deeper into river catchments, whereas males are more likely to remain in estuaries, harbours and the lower reaches of rivers.

PAGE TWENTY-NINE. **Was she silvering?**—in the months before they begin their journey to Sargasso, European eels metamorphose into 'silver eels', the visible characteristics of which are: pelagic counter-shaded livery, a metallic sheen, long pectoral fins and very large eyes. **Julius foul-hooked**—because the digestive systems of silver eels are atrophied, they do not feed at all, although they sometimes lunge atavistically at baits. On this occasion the fish was foul-hooked, in one of the pectoral fins, if I remember correctly.

PAGE THIRTY-ONE. **Dark moon**—as eels are phototaxic, they seek to avoid even dim light, preferring to begin their migration on cloudy nights in the pitch-dark of the New Moon. **Slick with gleaming fat**—the silver eel is the gourmet's eel.

PAGE THIRTY-TWO. **Abandons her length to the current**—silver eels seem to migrate passively when possible, probably as an energy saving device, allowing themselves to be taken by the current or tide. In conditions of spate, this mode of travel can be very rapid.

PAGE THIRTY-THREE. Silver eels are commercially harvested by means of **fyke or wing nets**. The blades of **Archimedes Screw** and other hydro-electric plant (HEP) turbines (for example, at the Ardnacrusha

HEP on Ireland's river Shannon and the *eight* HEPs on Sweden's river Atran) kill and maim millions of migrating silver eels every year. **Trent Falls**—the turbulent confluence of the rivers Ouse and Trent between Faxfleet in Yorkshire and Alkborough in Lincolnshire. A **catadromous** fish is one that is born at sea, migrates to freshwater to live out most of its life cycle, and returns to the sea to breed.

PAGE THIRTY-FOUR. **Procellariid**—'tube-nose', the name given to birds of the petrel and albatross families because of the peculiar form of their nostrils, which, like the eel's, take the form of external tubes. **Imprinted geomagnetic memory**—elvers imprint the details of estuarine tidal currents in their brains, as a navigational aid. **Benthic**—pertaining to the bed or bottom of any body of water. European **sturgeon** were found in the rivers of the Humber catchment well into the twentieth century. They are extremely long-lived fish (up to and beyond 100 years) and with age they can become huge—records indicate that some captured individuals exceeded fifteen feet in length and it is thought that some fish may have reached twenty feet or even longer. Now on the verge of extinction, the only wild population, with a maximum of 800 individuals and probably far fewer, exists in the Gironde river system in south-west France. A captive breeding programme (Gironde sturgeon have not bred in the wild since 1994, because HEPs and other dams prevent them from migrating upriver to their redds) has enabled some limited reintroductions into the Dordogne, Garonne, the Dutch Rhine and the German Elbe & Oder. Sturgeon do not become sexually mature until they are ten or fifteen years old, so the outcomes of these reintroductions will not be known for decades. **Donna Nook** is an RAF base on the coast of North Lincolnshire where **Thunderbolt** attack aircraft test their weaponry on an offshore bombing range.

PAGE THIRTY-FIVE. The **Anguillocola nematode** (*Anguillocola crassus*) is a parasite that infests the swim bladders of eels, affecting their ability to control their buoyancy. The nematode also weakens the eel's immune system and causes other physiological problems. *Anguillocola crassus* was inadvertently imported to Europe from Eastern Asia in the swim bladders of imported ornamental fish; **benzoylecgonine** is a metabolite of cocaine found in the tissues of eels in the Thames catchment and in other rivers that flow through cities where the recreational use of cocaine is endemic. It causes hyperactivity, nervous disorders and ultimately death in eels.

PAGE THIRTY-SIX. Although descending silver eels are easily netted in rivers, very few have been caught at sea. Consequently, we know virtually nothing of the details of their oceanic migration. A few European silver eels have been caught as accidentals by fishermen in the Mediterranean and in the English Channel. One was caught off the Hebrides, in the stomach of a long-lined Mora (**googly-eyed cod**); others have been found off the coast of Ireland in the guts of black scabbardfish; one was found in the stomach of a sperm whale (**cachalot**) killed off the Azores by the Prince of Monaco in 1899. Eels tagged with data-loggers and released in the Atlantic off France and Ireland travelled at depths between 300 and 800 metres, where three of them were predated by toothed whales. The wreck of HMS **Affray** lies at the bottom of the English Channel, as does the **Piper Malibu** the Argentinian football player Emiliano **Sala** was travelling in when it crashed in January, 2019. **No synchronous … fish**—the little evidence we have suggests that European eels migrate at great depths in the mesopelagic, across vast areas of ocean. Accordingly, eels are unlikely to form dense shoals, even though tens or even hundreds of millions might be travelling at any given time.

PAGE THIRTY-SEVEN. **Xiphius, macrocephalus … architeuthis**—swordfish, sperm whale and giant squid, respectively. **Entorhinal**—the cortex entorhinalis is the part of the brain concerned with memory and navigation.

PAGE THIRTY-EIGHT. **Fifteen, twenty … twenty-five miles a day**—the precise route the European eel takes to the Sargasso is unknown, as is the speed at which it travels. For the purposes of the poem, I assume eels travel on the currents of the North Atlantic Gyre, picking up the circulation with the Azores Current. The speed of the currents of the Gyre is highly variable, but would allow efficient, semi-passive travel within the range of the speeds given in the poem. **Seawolves** are U.S. nuclear submarines.

PAGE THIRTY-NINE. **The cordon narrows … deep-spaced shoal**—I imagine the migratory eels beginning to travel in closer proximity as they close in on Sargasso, using scent to find each other prior to breeding. **Three or four million eggs**—only Atlantic cod (*Gadus* *morhua*) rival the European eel in terms of the sheer quantity of ova produced by a single female. **Recycling**—as eels get closer to Sargasso, their migration, or pelagic, livery almost certainly begins to change into a different, breeding livery. To effect this transformation, the metamorphosis eels are already undergoing intensifies, redirecting minerals and other resources from their bones, digestive systems and eyes into their reproductive organs, resulting in their bodies becoming floppy, rubberised and waterlogged. At the point of mating, they are already on the verge of death. **Eight months and six thousand fasting miles**—both the distance eels travel on their migrations and how long it takes them are disputed, with some recent research suggesting eels may take up to eighteen months to make their catadromous migration. Some speculate that eels from Northern Europe may never reach the Sargasso to breed, implying that the whole population is supported by returners from southern rivers.

PAGE FORTY. **Imprinted larval hippocampus**—the part of the brain in which the elver stores its magnetic memory map to Sargasso. **Heat and salinity fronts**—the eel's thermo- and halo-taxes help them recognise the warm, salty water of their breeding grounds.

PAGE FORTY-ONE. **Blood-red speckling … upstream salmon**—male European eels artificially brought to sexual maturity by hormone injections have taken on the livery described.

PAGE FORTY-TWO. **Rubberised veterans … females, girthy as pythons, four or five feet long**—while some male eels that set off to Sargasso are tiny, some of the females are very large indeed, including individuals of fifteen pounds or more. The heaviest European eel officially recorded was caught in the Orlik reservoir in the Czech Republic in 1987 and weighed fifteen pounds and seven ounces. Several unverified—but not necessarily unreliable—claims refer to individuals over six feet in length and weighing up to thirty pounds. The current British record is an 11lb 2oz fish, caught by Steve Terry, at Kingfisher Lake in Hampshire, in 1978. However, in July 2019, a 'potential British record' eel was captured on the River Thames at Richmond, in an electrofishing survey conducted by the Environment Agency. The eel was measured at four-and-a-half feet in length but was not weighed. Standard length/weight conversion techniques gave its weight as 12lb 10oz.

PAGE FORTY-THREE. **Dead and dying eels**—it is believed that all European eels die after mating and spawning, a supposition supported by the fact that every captive European eel that has been artificially brought to sexual maturity in an aquarium has died within hours of ejaculation/spawning. A forty-year-old female eel kept in the Maretarium aquarium at Kotka, Finland, 'spontaneously matured' in 2019, and died with a coelum packed with ripe eggs. **Red clays**—the seabed of the Sargasso is made up of a fine sediment called 'red clay'—at least partly comprised, one imagines, of the remains of incalculable numbers of dead eels.

PAGE FORTY-FOUR. **He stiffens … hokey-cokey**—the breeding livery and mating ritual of European eels has never been observed in the wild and the description here is based on laboratory observations, the livery and ritual of the closely related Pacific/Indian Ocean species *Anguilla japonica* (the Japanese eel) and *Anguilla marmorata* (the Giant mottled eel)—and imagination. Despite the monogamous ritual described in the poem, it is thought that both female and male anguillid eels can, and do, breed with multiple partners before they die.

PAGE FORTY-FIVE. **Archaea** is the name given to the epoch of geological time stretching from 2.5 to 4.0 billion years ago, during in which period life evolved on Earth. **Pleroma**—the irrepressible fullness of life on Earth.

/ˈiːlaɪ/

The poems of this sequence are set in, allude to, or are otherwise connected with the West Riding village of Ulleskelf. The village is located on the river Wharfe in the Barkston Ash wapentake, about two miles upstream from Tadcaster. The river at Ulleskelf is well-known for its coarse fishing, which is administered by the Leeds and District Amalgamated Society of Anglers. In the 1970s, the fishing at Ulleskelf was dominated by eels. Anglers fishing for the other coarse fish—including the flounder, dace, perch, roach, bream, chub, pike and barbel that also proliferated in the river—were often frustrated by the sheer number of eels taking their baits and swallowing their rigs. Eels were regarded as vermin, and were killed as soon as they were landed, generally by decapitation.

Between 1977 and 1981, I would typically fish at 'Ulle' two or three times a year—on the first Saturday of the coarse fishing season and once or twice during the school summer holidays. I'd typically go with three or four friends from a wider peer group of ten or twelve—all more expert anglers than me. We'd board the 6.25am Sheffield-York train at Moorthorpe to make the forty-minute journey, stopping at Pontefract Baghill, Sherburn-in-Elmet and Church Fenton before finally arriving at Ulleskelf. We were often the only travellers on that early morning train—except on the first Saturday of the season, when as many as forty or fifty excited anglers from South Kirkby and South Elmsall would assemble on the platform in a quasi-festive atmosphere, excited at the prospect of breaking their three-month bankside fast.

I never caught anything other than eels at Ulleskelf, even when my mates and everyone else on the bank were landing flatties, pike, dace, etc. The first one I ever caught bit me—I tell myself I've still got the scar. No-one else I knew had ever been bitten by an eel—it provided a kind of intimate, personal connection. Consequently, Ulleskelf became synonymous with eels for me. It also became synonymous with trouble—the farmers, landowners and commuters that made up the population of the village weren't keen on working-class kids from pit villages sullying their suburbo-feudal enclave with their yobbish lack of deference and imputed propensities for shop-lifting, vandalism, trespass and fishing without day-tickets. Aggro with farmers, bailiffs, ten-bob millionaires, coppers and gangs of other kids seemed to occur on every trip.

I gave up angling in the early 1980s, but in subsequent decades returned to Ulleskelf on a few occasions— to relive old times, walk the landscape and look for curlews' nests. I also began to take a wider interest in the village, its landscape and history. Among other things, I found out that Ulleskelf was named for Úlfr Thoroldsson, an 11th century Viking jarl with extensive holdings in the East and West Ridings of Yorkshire—Úlfr's-scylfe (Úlfr's-'shelving piece of land by the river'—less pedantically, Úlfr's-place)—and that the hamlet had once been the site of a commercial eel fishery. Given the latter, and my history with the village, I couldn't resist hypothesising an alternative etymology—Áll-scylfe (Eel-place). The name is given in Domesday as *Oleschel* and *Oleslec*. When, in 2018, I started thinking about eels again, my imagination began to roam back to those barely remembered Ulleskelf days, and it rapidly became inevitable that my experiences there would find their way into the poem—Állscylfe is the omphalos, the origin and anchor of my encounter with the European eel.

Infangtheof: sometime in the mid-11th century, **Úlfr** Thoroldsson was bereaved of his wife **Gunnwårar**. In her memory he had a sundial built and carved with the inscription quoted in the poem. The sundial is now set into the wall of the parish church of the East Riding village of **Aldbrough**. At about the same time Úlfr also donated the manor of Ulleskelf to York Minster, before setting off on a pilgrimage to **Jerusalem**, probably as part of the same process of mourning for his wife—and preparation for his own death. The **Lambwath** is the stream that runs through Aldborough. **Cynesige** was Archbishop of York 1051-1060. He was succeeded by **Ealdred**, but ultimately the manor fell into the possession of William the Bastard. An **Arlesey bomb** is a ledger (fishing weight).

Inglnz Dreamin: this poem gives an account of my first fishing trip to Ulleskelf, which probably took place on the first Saturday of the 1977 coarse fishing season. **Brandlings** are small red worms found in quantity in the gravels of sewerage **trickling filters. God Save the Queen** by the Sex Pistols and **The First Cut is the Deepest** by Rod Stewart were fighting it out at the top of the charts at the time of the trip.

Dads at Lads: all my mates' Dads were anglers, so they were inducted into fishing from an early age and had their own tackle. My Dad wasn't an angler, so I wasn't and hadn't. A **Euclid** was an earth-moving machine used to shape colliery spoil heaps.

The Leeds & District ASA: the organisation that manages angling on the river Wharfe.

WMC Crawl: the **Diamond Jubilee**, **Coronation**, **Empire** and **Pretoria** are Working Men's Clubs in the adjacent former pit villages of South Kirkby, Moorthorpe and South Elmsall. **Vicky**, **Bertie**, **Winnie** and **Fred** are Queen Victoria, King Edward VII, Winston Churchill and Field Marshall Lord Frederick Sleigh 'Bobs' Roberts, Earl of Kandahar, Pretoria & Waterford, Viscount St. Pierre, Knight of the Garter, Knight of Grace and Justice of the Order of St. John,

Order of the Black Eagle, Order of Merit and commander of the British forces in the second Boer War, where he invented the modern concentration camp, in which he interned Boer civilians, mostly women and children (able-bodied men were sent abroad), over 26,000 of whom perished from malnutrition and disease. **Austin & Compton Rickett** were MPs for the Osgoldcross parliamentary constituency (in which the three villages were located) during the 1890s/1900s. **Campbell-Bannerman** was Prime Minister in the period 1905-08. The **tent city on Donkey Lane** housed the families of striking miners evicted from their homes by the management of Frickley Colliery during the strike for union recognition in 1907. **Herbert Smith** was the representative of the Yorkshire Miners Association during the strike.

Any Other Business: from the minutes of the management committee of the Leeds and District Amalgamated Society of Anglers, which somehow seems to have taken on the character of Ulleskelf Parish Council.

/ˈstiːvnz/ *Rod:* **Zaphnath-Paaneah** is the name given to Joseph by Pharaoh in Genesis 41:45. **Nehushtan** is the name given in 2 Kings 18:4 to the Brazen Serpent which God instructed Moses to erect on a pole to serve as a cure ('euery one that is bitten, when he looketh vpon it, shall liue') for the Israelites who had been bitten by the 'fierie serpents' God had previously inflicted on them as a punishment for moaning (Numbers 21:6-9). Job 1:7 ends the poem.

The Barkstone Ash & Skyrac Volunteers was the name of the militia established in the adjacent wapentakes of Barkston Ash and Skyrac. Local magnate Sir Thomas **Gascoigne** was a Catholic baronet and Foxite Whig and, from 1798, the commander of the Volunteers. Charles **Howard**, the 11th Duke of Norfolk, was a Catholic and another Whig radical. He was dismissed from the Lord Lieutenancy of the West Riding (and thus from his post as supreme commander of the *county* militia) by the Hanoverian lunatic George III, after toasting 'the sovereign majesty of the people' (rather than the king) at a London dinner. William **Fitzwilliam**, the 4th Earl Fitzwilliam, was the anti-Foxite Whig and former Lord Lieutenant of Ireland who replaced Norfolk in the roles he was dismissed from. **John Reeves** was an 'ultra-Tory' anti-Jacobin who, in 1792, founded the Association for Preserving Liberty and Property against Republicans and Levellers. **Anton Drexler** founded the German Nazi party in 1919. **Bantry Bay** is where the invasion fleet of the French revolutionary general Louis Lazare **Hoche** foundered in 1796, having been sent by the National Assembly to support the uprising of United Irishmen led by Theobald **Wolfe Tone**. The **London Corresponding Society** was a radical organisation that sought parliamentary reform and perhaps revolution. **Fishguard** and **Killalla** are locations where French invasion forces landed in 1797 and 1798, respectively. **Otmoor** in Oxfordshire was the site of anti-enclosure riots in 1829-30. William Horsfall, owner of **Ottiwells Mill** near Huddersfield, was killed by the Luddite leader George Mellor in 1812. In Norse mythology, **Níðhǫggr** is the serpent who gnaws at the roots of Yggdrasil, the World-Tree.

Gibbets: **Bully Beef** was a character from the children's comic, *The Dandy*. **Lord Snooty** was a character from the children's comic, *The Beano*. **Bodie** and **Doyle** were the two main characters in the TV show, *The Professionals* (1977-1983). **Glen Brown** and **Alan Wilson** are gamekeepers jailed (in 2011 and 2019 respectively) for killing raptors and other protected wildlife. **Ben Rothman** led the mass trespass on Kinder Scout in 1932. **Alf Tupper** was the hero of the comic strip 'Tough of the Track' in the boys' comic, *The Victor*. **Charles 'Dead Shot' Keen** was a character in the comic strip 'Billy's Boots' in the boys' comic, *Tiger & Scorcher*. **Wolfie** and **Shirl** were characters in the TV show *Citizen Smith* (1977-1980).

The Bridge: on our fishing expeditions to Ulleskelf, we'd usually set up near the railway bridge.

Plum: the poem imagines the train crash that took place at Ulleskelf station on 24th November, 1906. Plum oversaw the building of the **Sarras-to-Akasha** railway in Sudan during the Gordon Relief Expedition, 1884-85, and was stationed in **Bombay** during the plague of the late 1890s. He was godfather to P. G. Wodehouse who was named after him.

The Ship was a riverside pub at Ulleskelf. It was demolished in the early 2000s. The site was reused for 'executive housing'.

John's & Sam's: the John Smith's and Samuel Smith's breweries are in Tadcaster, two miles upstream from Ulleskelf. Some of us believed that Ulleskelf's eels thrived on the beer effluent we assumed was disposed of in the river. The National Socialist brothers **Adolf** and **Rudolf Dassler** founded the sportwear firms Adidas and Puma, respectively. Jesse **Owens** and Carl Ludwig '**Luz**' Long were rivals in the long jump at the Berlin Olympics of 1936, where they became friends. Gunter Grass's novel, *The Tin Drum*, is alluded to in this poem and several others in the sequence.

Jimmy Deadbait is modelled on a famous scene from *The Tin Drum*.

The Serenade of the Black Dwarfs also draws on *The Tin Drum*. **The Land of Nod** is a hamlet near the former fenland-edge town of Holme-on-Spalding-Moor, East Yorkshire, about 25 miles due east of Ulleskelf.

Jimmy the Tiger: yet more references to *The Tin Drum*.

/ˈstiːvn ˈiːlaɪ/ is a puff is a kind of condensed mythic auto/biography.

Jörmungandr is a rendering of the Old Norse poem Hymiskvida and is set in a fishing pond near the South Yorkshire town of Stainforth, on the edge of the Yorkshire fen. Ernst Stavro **Blofeld** is a villain from the James Bond films. He has been played by several actors. I have Charles Gray in *Diamonds are Forever* in mind.

marvelous weraal origin story is a Stan Lee-esque account of how /ˈstiːvn ˈiːlaɪ/ became a were-eel.

The American Mink is straightforward enough.

The four component poems of *Bollwurz* (an old Swabian name for deadly nightshade) are set in the contemporary riverine landscapes of the four dark age battles of their titles. The battle of *Maisbeli* was fought between an English army led by **Hengist**, and British forces led by **Aurelius Ambrosius**, at the confluence of the rivers Don and Dearne near the modern town of Mexborough. Hengist, the English chieftain, was captured and executed at **Kaerconan** (Conisborough) by the British leader **Eldol**, at the instigation of his brother, Eldad, the Bishop of Gloucester. Aurelius had argued that the pagan Hengist should be shown Christian mercy, but lost the debate when Eldad cited the precedent of Samuel's execution of the Amalekite king Agag in 1 Samuel 15. Local tradition identifies the site of Hengist's burial as a mound in a private **back garden** on the hill above the battlefield.

Hengist looks down from his tump across the site of Earl Fitzwilliam's **Cadeby Main** Colliery, where eighty-seven colliers were killed in a series of gas explosions on 9th July, 1912, the day of a royal visit.

The battle of the river **Idle** (*Idlæ*), which took place just south of the modern town of Bawtry, was the East Anglian king **Rædwald's** successful attempt to secure his status as **Bretwalda** by destroying his Northern rivals, **Æthelfrith** of Northumbria and **Ceretic** of Elmet, and installing **Edwin** of Deira as his puppet king in the North. The **NCB** was the National Coal Board and the **NFU** is the National Union of Farmers. The **Scrooby Congregation** were Protestant separatists from the eponymous Nottinghamshire town who, in 1608, left England for Holland so they might be able to worship freely. Ultimately, many of them emigrated to the New World, some on the Mayflower. The Don & Idle river systems, and the extensive fenland of which they were a part, were destroyed by a process of canalisation, re-routing of channels and water removal which began in the 17th century and continues to this day. The landscape is now dominated by intensive agriculture, with relict patches of ings and bog surviving as nature reserves.

At the battle of Hatfield (*Hæðfeld*), which took place near the former confluence of the rivers Don and Idle, Edwin, by then king of Northumbria and an aspirant Bretwalda himself, was killed in a battle between his armies and the combined forces of Penda of Mercia and Cadwallon of Gwynedd. The dead were buried in 'the Lings', an area of land between the modern villages of Stainforth and Hatfield Woodhouse. Today there are several prisons and young offenders' institutes—Lindholme, Moorland, Hatfield Lakes, Hatfield YOI—in the area. As inside left for South Kirkby Boys, I played at **Hatfield Borstal** (today's YOI) on several occasions. **William Whitelaw** was British Home Secretary in the period 1979-1983. Izaak Walton's *The Compleat Angler* is gently burlesqued.

At the battle of *Winwædfeld* (which took place where the Roman road now known by specialists as M28b crossed the river Went (Winwæd) south of Pontefract, at the modern hamlet of East Hardwick), **Penda** was killed by Oswui of Northumbria. The evolution of eels in the primaeval **Tethys** ocean is imagined at the end of the poem. **Haplorrhini** are early primate ancestors of humans.

Quo Warranto? means 'by what warrant/authority?' Quo warranto hearings were established in England by the Plantagenet kings, who sought to force land and franchise owners to prove their rights and titles by producing evidence of lawful authorisation. The principle has passed into common law and is now used to challenge arbitrary exercise of power.

eely

epigraph: **hengikjǫptr**, 'hangjaw', the european eel.

forwryd: a **weraal** is a were-eel.

body of dark: **agarthi** and **schamballah** are the occult cities of the east in theosophical tradition. **caligo** (latin) is darkness. **lilitu** is lilith, the hebrew demoness.

behold the head of a traitor: **rasalhague** is the brightest star in the constellation of **ophiuchos**. the **cla** is the country landowners' association. **akasha** is the mystical dark matter of space and time in theosophy. a **mine o' serpents** was a firework.

porzana: a **powte** is a burbot. the song of the **spotted crake** is said to sound like a dripping tap.

bloodspoor: **the dead … release**. eels are often said to eat rotting carrion—'a maggoty dead cat' is sometimes asserted to be the fenland eel-trapper's bait of choice. however, eels prefer to eat live or freshly dead prey.

pull down thy vanity: **slub** was cheap military clothing for conscripts or militiamen. a **size 5 air bomb repeater** is a powerful explosive firework. **huitzilopochtli** is the aztec god of war.

the patience & faith of the saints: the **south pump** is a fishing pond at Frickley.

the cross of a frog: **crucified … blasphemy**. aleister crowley describes the ritual implied in liber lxx.

ex nihilo ad nihilum: the **aalmutter** is the viviparous blenny, a european marine fish that gives birth to live young. the elongated larvae fishermen found inside the female blenny's coelom were once thought to be juvenile eels. current theories of the origin, nature and size of the universe depend on two hypotheses: firstly, that the spatial distribution of matter in the universe is homogeneous and isotropic (**the cosmological principle**) and, secondly, that **natural laws** are invariable throughout space-time. **baryogenesis** is the asymmetry that developed in the very early stages of the big bang, creating an imbalance of matter and anti-matter and thus providing the conditions for there to be something rather than nothing. the **coypu** is a large, semi-aquatic, south american rodent that was imported to england in the 20th century to be farmed for its fur. escapees established a feral population of close to half-a-million, which was systematically exterminated during the 1980s. the **hadalpelagic** is the deepest and darkest oceanic zone. an **eelpout** is a burbot.

moira: this poem rewrites some risqué playground songs and alludes to four types of durex rubber johnny. the **cmb** is the cosmic microwave background, the **ripple** which constitutes the evidence for baryogenesis.

10^{-43}: **macs0647-jd** is the oldest galaxy detectable from earth. located in the constellation camelopardalis (or **giraffe**), it was formed only 427 million years after the big bang and is over 300 billion light years distant. **livyatan** is an extinct species of sperm whale.

i do in all honesty love this world: the **hale-bopp** comet last visited earth in 1996/97. comets are formed in the region of space known as the **oort cloud**. **ymir** is the primaeval giant of norse mythology. the heavens were made from his skull. comets release vapours as they travel, a process known as **outgassing. panspermia** is the theory that life is seeded throughout the universe by means of comets. **acrosome, nucleus, middle-piece** and **tail** are the main parts of a spermatozoon. the **coma** is the atmosphere of a comet. photographs of the **hale-bopp** comet appeared to show an object travelling within its coma. some of these images were **doctored** by oddballs to give the impression that the object was an alien spaceship. members of the heaven's gate cult committed mass suicide—overdosing on **phenobarbital** dissolved in **applesauce**—as the comet approached earth, believing that their liberated souls would be taken by the spaceship to **telah**— 'the evolutionary level above human'. **auðumbla** is the primaeval cow of norse mythology who licked búri, the grandfather of the aesir, from the rocks.

jubilee: **thriddings** are the ridings of yorkshire.

ararita: **osiris** was killed and dismembered by his brother **seth**. he was revivified and reassembled by isis and anubis. the **cremaster** is the part of the chrysalis that attaches to a plant or other surface.

Eelysium

Eeliptical Fencentricities: the *Storegga* event was a series of landslips on the submarine Norwegian continental shelf that took place around 8000 years ago, causing the tsunamis that inundated Doggerland, carved out the English Channel and formed the North Sea. **'Oumuamua** was the first object of interstellar origin to be recognised as such as it passed through the Solar System (in 2017). The name means 'scout' in Hawaiian. Its shape is reminiscent of a severed eel head. A **Lipizzaner** is the dressage horse of Spanish Riding School, Vienna. Lipizzaners are trained when **longed**—tethered, orbiting around the trainer. Milutin Milanković (1879-1958) was a Yugoslavian climate scientist who discovered the cosmic and solar cycles that govern the fluctuations in Earth's climate—the so-called **Milankovitch** Cycles. Prior to the Storegga event, all the rivers that now empty into the English Channel and North Sea were tributaries of the **Rhine**, including the **Fleuve Manche**, or Channel River. The **Río de Oro** is a river in Western Sahara. **Eustatic** sea level rise is caused by the melting of the polar icecaps. A **whaup** is a curlew. A **butterbump** is a bittern.

Elverkonge means 'Elf-King' in Danish, and Goethe's 'Erlkönig' lurks in the background of this poem. However, it was the double-eeliness of the name that drew me to it. **Maremmana** are an ancient breed of cattle, still extant in Italy, closely related to the extinct aurochs; by extension, Maremmana is cheese made from the breed's milk.

Morimarusa (the Dead Sea) was the Latinised version of the name given to the North Sea by the Germanic tribes of North-West Europe in the Roman period. **Brigantes … Trinovantes**—British tribes having territory that bordered the Mori Maru. **Frisi … Morini**—Gaulish and Germanic tribes having territory bordering the Mori Maru. **Nehalennia** was a Celtic-German goddess worshipped in Zeeland around 2000 years ago, propitiated by those trading across the Morimaru. The so-called 'Pillar of the Boatmen' was a Romano-Gaulish sculpture erected by the boatmen of **Lutetia** (Paris) in the first century AD. The pillar displayed representations of the deities **Cernunnos**, **Smertrios** and **Tarvos Trigaranos**. The pillar, and a replica, are displayed in the Musée de Cluny. **Publius Quinctilius Varus** was the commander of the three Roman legions annihilated by a coalition of German tribes in the Teutoberg Forest in 9AD. **Albruna** is a seeress mentioned in Tacitus' *Germania*. The **Ninth Hispana** was a Roman legion stationed in Britannia. The legion seems to have disappeared in the early second century and some speculate that it was wiped out in an undocumented uprising of Britons. I imagine the legion meeting its end at the hands of the Brigantes in the fenlands between Doncaster (**Danum**) and Tadcaster (**Calcaria**). **In middan Girwan fænnen** ('in the middle of the fen belonging to the Gyrwe') is a phrase from Bede's *Ecclesiastical History of the English People*. According to the Tribal Hidage, the Gyrwe were the Anglo-Saxon people that inhabited the Cambridgeshire/South Lincolnshire fen. **Freyr** ... **Odin**—the fenland was part of the Danelaw. The Modern English word 'Lord' is derived from the Old English 'Hlaford', or **Loaflord**—thus 'Lords' are a species of Cain.

The Enthronement Feast of Archibishop George Neveel was catered for according to the list in the text box (adapted from John Leland's *Antiquities of Great Britain*, 1533-36, 1774 Thomas Hearne edition), a fantastic fenland harvest testifying to the superabundance of the habitat. **Savile** ... **Jenkyns**—a rogues' gallery of Yorkshire right-wingers attended the feast, apparently. **Ahuitzotl** introduced the **great-tailed** grackle to the fenland around Teotihuacan, after the native **slender-billed** grackle had been extirpated from the marshes. Grackle feathers were used in high-status Aztec war-cloaks. **Huia** were a species of New Zealand bird that became extinct in 1907. Their feathers were also used in high-status (Maori) cloaks, but it was the British that finally did for them. Lake **Titicaca** is a freshwater lake on the Bolivian/Peruvian border that is/was the habitat for many endangered and extinct species, including the flightless Titicaca grebe and the Titicaca water frog. **Euhemerus of Rhodes** provided banal demythologising accounts of the Greek Myths. The fenland of

Thorne Moor held a population of **wolves** into the Early Modern period. The hybrid Latin/Spanish phrases in italics are from the Our Father. **Centeotl** was the Aztec maize deity. **Tiddy Mun** ('Little Man') was the name given to the *genius loci* of the fen by the islanders of Axholme.

Girvij, or closely related terms derived from 'Gyrwe', were used to identity the Cambridgeshire and south Lincolnshire fenfolk into the modern period.

Eeldorado: the **naughty paike** of *Eelizardbirth* is Anne Boleyn. She raised and hand-fed dotterels which she kept as pets—before she had them strangled and prepared as dainties. **O death rock me asleep** is a Tudor-era poem, often attributed to Boleyn—said to have been written by her during her imprisonment, as she waited to be executed. Boleyn's daughter, the future Queen Elizabeth I, **came out red**, and eventually supplanted her equally red sister, Mary I, just as Jacob supplanted his red brother Esau in Genesis 26. At the battle of **Flores** in 1592, a small fleet of privateers led by **Sir Walter Raleigh** boarded and looted the Portuguese treasure ship **Madre de Deus**. State-sponsored piracy was a major source of Royal income, and the Queen (and her courtiers) would routinely invest in piratical expeditions, as they promised huge returns for minimal outlay. **Francis Drake** died of dysentery during an abortive 1596 raid on Spanish treasure ships in the Caribbean. His last words were **we must have gold**—to give the Queen a good return on her investment so that he might remain in her favour and keep his head. The **Dutch Republic** developed the earliest form of joint stock capitalism, at least partly related to the need to collectively invest in their sea defences and to drain and convert their fenlands to profitable farmland—as well as to mitigate the risk associated with exploiting their Batavian colonies. **Dogs** and **beggars** were Dutch mercantile ships. The English looked with envy at Dutch profit margins and developed their own proto-colonial trading monopolies in the **East Indies**, **Cathay** and **Muscovy** on Dutch models. It was during the battle of **Zutphen** in 1586 that William **Russell**, later appointed Governor of Flushing, came up with the idea to drain the Bedford Level, having seen similar works in Holland produce fertile farmland capable of giving an annual return of 10%. Russell subsequently contracted with several

Dutch adventurers & undertakers (venture capitalists and drainage engineers)—including **Pedersen**, **Jacobsen** & **Alert**—to begin the drainage of the Bedford Level of the Cambridgeshire fen. Roy **Lynk** was the leader of the strikebreaking Nottinghamshire miners during the 1984/5 Miners' Strike. Arthur **Scargill** was the leader of the National Union of Mineworkers in the same period. David **Hart** was the Old Etonian multi-millionaire who effectively led the Government's attempts to break the strike. Hart died in 2011 and is interred in a pyramid in the grounds of Chadacre Hall, his Suffolk country house. **She wyrm** … **mutton**—these lines describe Elizabeth's physical condition at her time of death; **braxie** mutton comes from sheep that die from disease or natural causes—effectively carrion. **All my possessions for a moment of time** were the basilisk Queen's deeply ambiguous last words. **Drakon** is a Russian algorithmic programming language used by speculators and hedge funds to make investment decisions.

The *Baseeliske* is James VI of Scotland/I of England. **A pockish man, I could have died of his breath** is how James' mother, Mary, Queen of Scots, described the syphilitic Lord Darnley, his father. Mary also identified the Archbishop of St. Andrews, who presided over her son's baptism, as 'pockish', and thus refused to allow him to spit into the mouth of her son (then part of the baptismal ceremony). The italic lines beginning **Mary had a baby** are a rendering of the opening verse of a playground song popular in South Kirkby in the mid-1970s. The **witches of North Berwick** were prosecuted by James VI in 1590.

Corneelius satirises the **money for nothing** ethos of the adventurers and undertakers who sought to drain the fen, with some help from Dire Straits. It also satirises the obsequious 'patriotic' eagerness of the English to honour the historical celebrities about whom they know so little. **Anton Mussert** was the leader of the Nationaal-Socialistische Beweging in Nederland, the Dutch Nazi Party. He held Nuremberg-style rallies in the Dutch town of **Lunteren**, where he began to build a parade ground on the model of the Luitpoldarena. He was executed as a traitor by his countrymen in 1946. **Sutcliffe** is Peter, the Yorkshire Ripper. The **Three Amigos** were Brendan Batson, Laurie Cunningham and Cyrille Regis, the three outstanding black players who broke into the West Bromwich Albion first team in the late 1970s and who are honoured outside the Hawthorns with a statue by Barnsley sculptor Graham Ibbeson. The slaver Edward Colston's statue was thrown in Bristol Harbour in 2020 as part of the Black Lives Matter protests.

The Royal Forest of *Hatfield Chace* was at the heart of the Yorkshire/North Lincolnshire fen. **Syzygy** is the alignment of Sun, Moon and Earth that causes the springtides. The collision of these high tides in the looping and braided Don system (with tides entering the various channels of the river from the Trent in the East and the Aire in the West, with both tides meeting 'in the middle' near Thorne) is thought by some to have been a major cause of the region's regular inundation. **Ombrotrophic** mire is raised peat bog, fed by rainwater. Thorne Moor, adjacent to Hatfield, was one of the largest ombrotrophic bogs in lowland England until it was destroyed by commercial peat extraction in the 20th century. **Sir Philibert Vernatti, Lucas van Valkenburg, Martijn Corselis** and **Jacob Cats** were Dutch courtiers, adventurers and undertakers who invested in the drainage of Hatfield Chase and the Isle of Axholme. The Leveller Thomas **Rainsborough** was killed in Doncaster marketplace on 29th October, 1648, during a bungled royalist kidnap attempt. He had travelled to the town by boat along the Humber system and, like many radicals, opposed the drainage and enclosure of the fens. The quotations in the text boxes are taken from Charles Jackson's 1870 edition of *The Diary of Abraham de la Pryme* (written 1683-1704).

The Great Leveel is the Bedford Level of the Cambridgeshire Fen, ultimately drained and enclosed by Vermuyden in partnership with Francis **Russell**, the 4th Earl of Bedford. **Argus** refers to the Large Copper butterfly (the 'Orange Argus of Elloe'), which once thrived in the southern fenlands, but became extinct after the drainage. The **Dutchman** in this case is William of Orange. Under Charles I and subsequent Stuart kings, the fenland was 'planted' with settlers thought likely to be loyal to the Protestant Crown—and to the Crown's practice of drainage and enclosure—in a way in which the expropriated and dispossessed natives were not: a similar colonial model to that deployed by James I in Ulster, although in the fenland the planted population was predominantly Dutch and Huguenot rather than northern English and Scots. The Argus looks down on the superabundant fen and sees an **ant-line voortrek**: these are refugees from the Axholme town of Sandtoft, near Hatfield Chase, a planted settlement of eighty Dutch and Huguenot families. On 18th October, 1651, the town was sacked and the settlers driven out by commoners led by the prominent Levellers John Lilburne and John Wildman, with local men Richard Raw and Daniel Noddel. The expelled settlers fled to a similar Dutch colony at Thorney, Cambridgeshire. They returned to Sandtoft a few years later, as the English Revolution gradually succumbed to the reaction that would culminate in the Restoration and ultimately the debacle of 1688-90. The **Royal William** is the swallowtail butterfly, *Papilio machaon*, named for Machaon, surgeon to the Greeks at Troy, on account of the lancet-like spurs on its wing. The swallowtail was brought to the edge of extinction by the drainage. The **Whittel Sea** was a Cambridgeshire fenland lake, six square miles in area. It was progressively drained from the 17th century and now no longer exists. **Heorot** stands for the British and other Museums (and by extension the British State) in which artefacts plundered from the Empire and the natural world are stored and displayed. Rory O'Donnell, 1st Earl of **Tyrconnell**, fled Ulster in 1607, along with his neighbour Hugh O'Neil, 2nd Earl of Tyrone, in the so-called 'flight of the Earls', when it became clear that James I was about to have them both arrested for treason. Their Ulster estates defaulted to the Crown. James promptly sold them off and settled the land with Protestant loyalists to secure his windfall. **Pat Finucane** was an Irish solicitor assassinated by the British State in collusion with Loyalist paramilitaries in 1989.

Eelimentary Tractaet van Dijckagie: Tractaet van Dijckagie was a 16th century manual on fen drainage written by Andries Vierlingh. *Tyranipocrit* takes its title from *Tyranipocrit Discovered*, a revolutionary Leveller pamphlet published anonymously in Rotterdam in 1649. **Knútr** was the Danish king of England, Denmark and Norway in the period 1016-1035. Several apocalyptic Dutch floods (for example those of 1219, 1362 and 1634) were given the name **die grote mandränke** ('the big drowner'). The **Sermo Lupi ad Anglos** (Sermon of the Wolf to the English) was given by Wulfstan, Archbishop of York, around the time of the Danish invasion of 1014 (led by Knútr's father, and his predecessor as king of the English, Sweyn Forkbeard). Wulfstan argued that the advent of the Northmen was the result of corruption and moral laxity among the English ruling classes. **Prerogative ανομία** is the essential lawlessness at the heart of Monarchy and the Divine Right.

Balby Carr Pastoreel is set between the eponymous **Balby Carr** (Doncaster—formerly part of the Yorkshire fen) and the M18 motorway. The italics in lines 7-9 & 21-22 are taken from 19th century folk rhymes. A **PRU** ('prue') is a Pupil Referral Unit (where children permanently excluded from mainstream schools are contained). **Hatfield**, in this case, refers to the Young Offenders Institute. **Associate** is the name Amazon gives to its warehouse workers. **Donny/Dee-Dah Airport** is the now defunct Doncaster-Sheffield Airport, at Finningley, on the edge of the former Yorkshire fen. Dee-Dah is a contemptuous South Yorkshire insult directed at Sheffielders, who notoriously pronounce the 'th' in the Yorkshire dialect 'thee' and 'tha' as 'd'.

Privy Counceel—**Titbits** was a salacious weekly newspaper that ran from 1881 to 1984. A **Mega Luv Doner** is a spectacular kebab. **Robin Asquith** is the actor who played the titular cockney Jack-the-Lad in the 1974 sex comedy, *Confessions of a Window Cleaner*. The death of another king, on the lavatory, eating a hamburger, in his mansion of spongers and sycophants, haunts the poem.

The title of *Sea-worm* is taken from and alludes to Ted Hughes's poem 'Mayday on Holderness', his manifesto-like characterisation of the Universe as a system of devouring. **Orecchio negro**—'black ears' is an Italian name for the silver eel, the ears in question actually being the elongated pectoral fins of the eel in migration livery. **Chiasmodon niger**, the Black swallower, is a small deep-sea fish whose external stomach is elastic and extendable, enabling it to devour and digest prey much larger than itself. **Cestodes, hairworms, flukes, hooks** and **enterobes** are intestinal parasites. **O white devil, Tyranipocrit, how impious thou art**, is an appropriation from *Tyranipocrit Discovered*.

The *Commissioners of Sewers* were bodies appointed from the ranks of the nobility, other major landowners and relevant State representatives to oversee drainage in any given area. They played a major—and often legally questionable and deeply corrupt—role in the drainage and enclosure of the fens. **Sir William Killigrew** was a slaver, fen drainer, dramatist, poet and financial schemer. From 1660 he was Vice-Chamberlain to Queen Henrietta Maria. He was the architect of a bond scheme which he advertised as likely to provide **vast gains** to investors.

Eelkonoklastes alludes to John Milton's *Eikonoklastes*, the extended essay in which he justifies the execution of Charles I in response to the latter's *Eikon Basilike*. *Filth as thou art* is the aristocratic Prospero's contemptuous remark to his servant Caliban in *The Tempest*. The second stanza of the poem alludes to the 1993 Haximu massacre in the Brazilian Amazon, when a group of **garimpeiros** (gold miners) slaughtered several **Yanomami** and burned down their village. **Haxi** is a township on the Isle of Axholme. The calculatedly deployed exhibitionist racism of Alexander Boris de Pfeffel Johnson, the fifty-fifth Prime Minister of the United Kingdom of Great Britain and Northern Ireland, is alluded to and partially quoted in the lines, **panga wielding paki / ninnies, watermelon smiles. Rita, Sue and PetSu too** alludes to Andrea Dunbar's 1982 play *Rita, Sue and Bob Too* and Alan Clarke's identically named 1987 film of the play. **PetSu** is Peter Sutcliffe. **Jayne MacDonald** was a sixteen-year-old schoolgirl murdered by Sutcliffe in 1977. **Spinnefix** ('Quick Spider') was the nickname given by SS guards to Simon Srebnik, a thirteen-year-old Polish Jew who was deported to the **Kulmhof** (Chelmno) killing centre with his family in 1942. Srebnik's family was exterminated in the gas vans on arrival, but he was put to work gathering fodder for the camp rabbits. Hearing him sing Polish folk songs such as Mały Biały Domek (**Little White House**) as he completed his work, the SS guards taught him Nazi marching songs, such as The Black Band of **Florian Geyer**. Srebnik was one of only seven survivors of Kulmhof. In January 1945, two days before the Red Army liberated the camp, he was taken by the SS and made to stand in the headlights of a staff car so that he might be seen better to be shot. He smashed the headlights and ran. Srebnik made good his escape (despite having a bullet in his head) and survived with the help of Polish farmers. He eventually settled at **Ness Ziona** in Israel. Ness has been the author's nickname for much of his life. The penultimate stanza gives an account of an ideological graffito Ness scrawled in the endpapers of a Brer Rabbit book on 10th November, 1974 at the age of nine, whilst watching Sheffield United beat Luton one-nil on Sunday Soccer. A **Bog-bull** is a bittern. In 1638, a group of 600 fen-folk assembled to 'play football' at **Whelpmore Fen**, near Ely, Cambridgeshire. In fact, the football match was a pretext and they proceeded to tear down the sluices, drainage dykes and marked-out plots of the undertakers.

The Thorne Moor landscape of the opening stanza of *Grendeel* is now surrounded by a forest of wind turbines. Until 2004, when they were demolished, ultimately to make way for a solar farm, the twin towers of the Thorne Colliery **winding gear** dominated the landscape and provided a useful orientation point for those lost on the flat and landmark-less moor. **Regnum defende** is the motto of **MI5**. **Semper occultus** is the motto of **MI6**. **Hughes** is Francis, one of several IRA volunteers from Seamus Heaney's hometown of Bellaghy. Hughes was at large and on the run in the boglands of Mid-Ulster for several years before his capture in a gunfight with the British Army in 1978. He was imprisoned in the 'H' Blocks at Long Kesh, where, on 12th May, 1981, he became the second of ten Republican prisoners to die on hunger strike in that year. Robert **Nairac** was the Ampleforth, Oxford, Sandhurst and Trinity College educated British army officer who conspired with loyalist paramilitaries (the 'Glennane Gang') to bomb Dublin and commit sectarian murders of Catholics. He was implicated in the murder of Heaney's cousin Colum McCartney at **Altnamachin** on 25th August, 1975 and in the Miami Showband massacre of 31st July in the same year. Brian **Nelson**, another British agent, colluded with loyalist paramilitaries to commit dozens of sectarian murders, including that of Pat Finucane. **William Bunting** led the 1970s/80s grassroots direct-action campaign that saved Thorne Moor from being turned into a landfill or airport, ultimately leading to its designation as a National Nature Reserve—establishing himself as an unlikely ecowarrior-hero in the process. A single-minded and confrontational character, Bunting had previously fought with the International Brigades during the Spanish Civil War and worked undercover for the Special Intelligence Service in the Second World War. In 2015, his reputation was irreparably damaged when it was revealed that he had sexually and physically abused several members of his family, including his wife, daughters and granddaughters. A **shoggoth** is a huge, protoplasmic, amoeba-like creature in H.P.

Lovecraft's Cthulhu mythos. Tacitus' description of the role and behaviour of Germano-Celtic women in battle, in both the *Agricola* and the *Germania*, is incorporated into the description of the fen women's contribution to the resistance to the drainers. Robert **Coggan** was shot dead by the militia during a protest against drainage and enclosure in Axholme. The penultimate stanza alludes to Lovecraft's 'The Shadow Over Innsmouth', in which marine beings of extra-terrestrial origin couple with humans, creating a hybrid race of sinister fish-people. The section **Heretics … wickerman's hurdle** alludes to Tacitus's account in the *Germania* of the method used by Teutonic tribesmen to execute those they considered sexual deviants. On the Micronesian island of **Pohnpei**, the Lasialap clan regard the Giant mottled eel (*Anguilla marmorata*) as a totem. The eels are venerated and fed with tinned fish and **dog food**. Many of these eels become so tame, they are willing to rise from the water to take food from hand.

The Black Mirror is a perfectly circular, bottomless well located in a cotton grass quagmire on Hatfield Moor. **William Torksey** was a leader of the resistance to the drainage in the Hatfield area in the 1630s. **Askr, tade, grig**—newt, toad, eel. The **Magus** is the spirit of William of Lindholme, a 14th century hermit, mystic and magician ('Prospero of the Fen', according to Charles Jackson, in a note in *The Diary of Abraham de la Pryme*), who Torksey has had the Widow conjure from the world of the dead in much the same way that Saul had the Witch of Endor conjure the wraith of the prophet in 1 Samuel 28:3-25. De la Pryme was a second-generation Huguenot settler and his family home near Thorne was previously the residence of the man he deferentially referred to as 'Mijn Heer' **van Valkenburg** even decades after the latter's death. The **aegre** is the tidal bore on the river **Trent**. Common **cranes** have now found their way back to the regenerating post-industrial landscapes of Thorne and Hatfield moors.

The Ruin of Heorot—in this poem Heorot is **Sandtoft**. In November 1641, dispossessed Ulstermen rose up and massacred around a hundred of the planted English and Scottish settlers of **Portadown**. Ten years later, after the expulsion of the Dutch/Huguenot settlers from Sandtoft, **Freeborn John** Lilburne, the Leveller leader who had been contracted to lead the fenfolk's fight for the restoration of their land and rights, took up residence in the Pastor's house and used the Dutch/French chapel as a barn for his cattle. His message to the settlers is quoted in full in the final two lines of the poem. **Nemmersdorf** and **Königsberg** are sites of massacres of German civilians perpetrated by Red Army soldiers in the final year of World War Two.

Suspiria Regalia ('The Sighs of the King') was the original title of Charles I's *Eikon Basilike*, the self-justification he wrote, or had ghosted, in the lead up to his execution. **Big Fish Eat the Little Fish** is a 1557 engraving by the Flemish artist Pieter van der Heyden. **Earth's crown, crown of thorns, starrie crown of glorie** are terms used by Charles I to describe the evolution of his various 'crowns' (triumph, suffering, martyrdom) in *Eikon Basilike*. A number of other phrases from the work are appropriated and worked into stanza two. **Fari vagnari u pizzu**—the classic preamble of the Sicilian mafia extortioner—'please, allow me to wet my beak'. **The whole inheritance / deemed as waste that the rampant Crown / might seize it**—some courtier groups, aware that 'waste'—Royal Forest, such as Hatfield—was wholly owned by the king, and that he was not accountable to anyone for the way in which he disposed of it, explored ways in which the king might declare the whole of the country Royal Forest, so there might be a generalised redistribution, from which he and they might 'vastly gain'. This abortive idea was predicated on the prerogative absolutism of the Divine Right and the concomitant elimination of Parliament and any systemic checks on Royal power. **John Cook** led the prosecution of Charles I. **John McMichael** was a leader of the Ulster Defence Association. His victims were beaten and killed in so-called **Romper Rooms**. Charles II's Act of **Oblivion** (Indemnity and Oblivion Act, 1660) granted an amnesty to all those implicated in the Parliamentarian struggle against the Crown, apart from fifty named seditionaries and regicides, nine of whom were executed. Three corpses were also dug up and violated.

Enuma Eelysh envisages the restoration of the fen following apocalyptic flooding caused by anthropogenic global warming. *Gods of Storm & Abyss* does so by drawing on the flood-narrative in the *Epic of Gilgamesh*. The topography of the landscape of Eastern England after any significant rise in sea level would result in a naturally restored fen stretching from **Huntingdon to York**.

The Burbots of Guthlac—**Peny of Wisbech** wrote The Powte's Complaint in 1619. The poem, written in the imagined voice of a powte, or **burbot**, is a remarkably prescient piece that anticipates and protests the planned and imminent drainage of the Cambridgeshire/Lincolnshire fen—and predicts the social and ecological impacts of the drainage. In the poem I conflate Peny with Guthlac, the 7th/8th century Saint and hermit of Crowland and present the composite figure as a latter-day William of Lindholme, using magick to thwart the drainers. **Little sister of the fen / thou hast been meddling in the Goetia** is a rendering of Alan Bennett's remark to Aleister Crowley at their first meeting. Peny invokes the **Ancient Water Nurses** in The Powte's Complaint. **Lota lota** is the burbot. **Holastri, Nimorup, Nominon … the 49 servitors of Beelzebub** were demons conjured by Crowley in his pursuit of the Great Work of securing his Holy Guardian Angel by conducting the rituals of Abramelin the Mage. I imagine Guthlac deploying his imps against the Elizabethan magus John Dee, who lived at **Mortlake** on the Thames and one of whose works, **Hydragogy**, advocated the drainage of the fens. **Tupny Jack** is a pike from Peny's poem. The poem closes with a vision of an antediluvian, restored fen that draws on the flood narratives of Genesis and the *Epic of Gilgamesh*, and ends with a paraphrase of God's comments in Genesis 8:21.

Pantaneel presents a vision of a restored Yorkshire/Lincolnshire fen around Axholme and Hatfield Chace after Apocalyptic flooding has eliminated humans from the landscape. The **temple** in the first stanza is St. John the Baptist Church, Alkborough. The **filídh** are poets in the Gaulish/Celtic tradition. **Freyja** had a cloak of falcon feathers. **Wieland** the Smith made himself some mechanical wings and attempted to fly. The **Fina** oil refinery is at Killingholme on the Humber estuary. **Amitsoq gneiss** is a type of rock found off Greenland, where some **Atlantic salmon** feed. **Pigfish** are porpoises. **Trident** is the UK's submarine-launched nuclear missile programme. The **Brier** was the name given to the main southern channel of the Don (the Don formerly braided into three courses near Thorne, with the two southern channels travelling east to empty into the Trent at Adlingfleet and Luddington, and the northern channel joining the Aire near Snaith). In 1629, Vermuyden channelled all the waters of the Don into the northern branch, which he canalised (creating the so-called 'Dutch River') and diverted into the Ouse at Goole. A **gime** is a deep pond created by the scouring action of a river overflowing its banks. **Anax imperator** is the Emperor dragonfly. **Eelfare**—a run of elvers up the river.

Dreams of Sturgeon—before its relocation to the new Danum Gallery complex on the Waterdale, Doncaster Museum & Art Gallery, which possesses the stuffed carcasses of two locally caught sturgeon, was located on **Chequer Road**. A sturgeon's caudal (tail) fin is **heterocercal**, meaning that the upper part is longer than the lower, like a shark's. The knobbly plates that run along a sturgeon's back and flanks are known as **scutes**.

Πάντα Ρεελ—a rendering of Plato's summary (in Cratylus) of the key tenet of Heraclitus's philosophy—'everything flows'—or everything is the eel. The section, **the net brake ... will hee giue him a snake?**, is a conflation of Luke 5:6 and Matthew 7.

Acknowledgements

Thanks are due to Dr Matthew Gollock, Marine and Freshwater Programme Manager at the Zoological Society of London; Dr Bram Houben, Wildlife Biologist at ARK Natuurontwikkeling; Paul Kemp, Professor of Ecological Engineering at the University of Southampton; and Pete Wall, Nature Recovery Manager at Sheffield & Rotherham Wildlife Trust, each of whom contributed enormously to the understanding of the European eel that informs the opening movement. I am also indebted to my friends and colleagues Michael Stewart and Ed Reiss, who each commented helpfully on early drafts of the book, and Todd Borlik, who introduced me to Peny of Wisbech and Tiddy Mun, and shared with me his wide knowledge of fen-related literature.

Some sections of the poem have previously been published elsewhere. An earlier version of 'Eel' was published by Longbarrow Press as *The European Eel* (2021) with artwork by P.R. Ruby. 'Commissioners of Sewers' was included in the Grist anthology, *We're All In It Together* (2022). 'Eeliptical Fencentricities' was published in the *Fenland Poetry Journal*. 'John's & Sam's' and 'Jörmungandr' were published in the *London Review of Books*. 'Maisbeli' was published in the *Times Literary Supplement*.